Turn Your Rural Property into a Wedding Venue Business

A How-to Guide for Earning Thousands of Dollars from Your Home on Weekends

AMEÉ QUIRICONI

ISBN: 9798580664460

DEDICATION

This book shows that even if things don't go as planned, sometimes you find out that's even better.

So, this book is dedicated to anyone looking for a fresh start.

TABLE OF CONTENTS

ACKNOWLEDGMENTS

I want to thank all of the readers from the first version that wrote to me and shared their stories and feedback! It has been so encouraging to see you all follow your dreams!

And thank you to Sharon St. Marie, my best friend who also helped ensure my typos didn't undermine me on this second round. I can't think of anyone who deserves more to be a part of this "Re-Do" than you.

1
A RE-INTRODUCTION

As my dedication hinted, this book is about re-dos.

First, I'm updating this book based on the questions and comments I received from past readers to the original that deserve to be included. And I'm punching up some of the sections on *marketing*, *branding*, and *money* because those are important when starting this business or any business venture. In fact, the content in those three areas alone is as much as the length of the entire first version of this book!

I also wanted to re-do the book because when I wrote it, it was less about the actual content and more about finally doing something I always dreamed of, which was being an author. That means I spent a lot of time working on the mechanics of self-publishing a book and overlooked or, more accurately, sped through some aspects of the writing and organization. Most of the readers forgave me and loved the book anyway, but a few critics were not shy about pointing the mistakes out. That's fair.

I also decided that the book needed an update because big, catastrophic things happened in the world in 2020 that crushed the wedding industry, for lack of a better word. Stay-at-home orders and bans on gatherings pretty much made any business that relied on bringing people together for celebrations illegal to operate for a while. Therefore, a book about wedding venues needed new information because while some things are the same, a new line of thinking needs to be brought to the venue industry based on what happened. Some pivots for venues were indeed temporary solutions to a current problem, but the pandemic did change all of us in a few ways that have to be considered moving forward.

In that same vein, this book could be about re-dos for some of you because of the pandemic. What I mean is that some of you may be looking at a home-based business like this because you became unemployed or had to leave your jobs. During the pandemic, the U.S. Census Bureau found that three times as many women as men left careers or scaled back their hours because of a lack of childcare. Women were also more likely than men in two-parent households to pick up the extra responsibilities of home-schooling their children until it was safe for in-person gatherings to happen again. This reduction in income has to be made up someplace. So, finding a financially stable job with a high degree of flexibility that somebody can also run from the kitchen table while kids are on a Zoom call with their teachers is an excellent option for many families.

But this book is also a re-do for me. A lot had changed in my life since 2016 when I initially published my book about starting a wedding venue business on your rural property. I wish I could say that in 2016, I had no idea of what was to happen just a year later. But if I said that, then I'd be lying to you and myself. I started working on that little book in 2016 because I felt the winds shifting and knew it was the beginning of the end. And I suppose I hoped that I could become an air-bender by capturing in writing the story of my romantic adventure into weddings because I fell in love with a guy and it would make everything okay. But instead of altering our fate, it only cemented it.

So, the partnership between two people and their rural wedding venue business ended that I wrote about in 2016 ended. And not because of the company itself but because of the deeper, inner turmoil that humans struggle with. And so, I needed to reopen this chapter of my life, reflect on it a bit, and bring the perspective we all gain once we are through with the journey and we look back. The book needed to be rewritten to add finality to that leg of my trip into weddings.

I withdrew from the wedding venue business in 2018 and entered a new phase of mental health, self-improvement, and parenting. I unraveled my personal history and removed the scaffolding around me I erected to protect me from abuse. I had lived many years believing that I was "okay" when it became clear in 2017 I was far from it.

Life, however, is not a straight line from point A to point B. We all know that. It's not even a zigzag or a scribble. Sometimes it's more like edging along the surface of a coil, moving forward, and circling back around simultaneously. So, it wasn't a surprise that after a couple of years of focused work on psychology, neuroscience, and human behavior, I would come back to my other real passion: entrepreneurship.

During this time, I was still coaching businesses, including several wedding venues around the country. I noted that what kept me from turning a corner in my professional life was not just my problem. There was something pretty universal about why some business owners make it and some don't. Why do some people create businesses and lifestyles that give them true financial freedom, and why do some people continue to live paycheck to paycheck.

So, I eased myself back into the wedding business lane again, this time armed with an arsenal of knowledge of nuclear proportions that I lacked before. And I knew, not decided, that my true purpose was to bring this knowledge I gained through failures and missteps to other entrepreneurs so that I could hopefully help prevent any heartaches that lay ahead of them.

So, will this book decode all those secrets for you? No. That is a different book. But this book does have some hints that anyone who goes into business for themselves or with a spouse or partner should initially be mindful. I still owe you that.

Before we dive in, let's see whether the wedding venue business is still a business to start. When I wrote and published my book in 2016, creating a wedding venue business was very different from today. But I believe it is still an excellent business to consider, especially for people with rural home properties. And here's why.

Weddings are still big business. According to WeddingWire.com, since 2016, the market has grown from a $54 to $74 billion industry in the United States. That's billions. With a "B!"

In WeddingWire's 2020 report, a survey of over 27,000 couples between January 1 and December 31, 2019, found that, on average, couples hire (15) vendors for their wedding day. And the most often hired vendor – you guessed it – The venue! Meaning, people opt out of some of the other services, but 92% of the couples surveyed still had a professional venue to host their big event.

What is also increasing is the venue rental fees. In 2016, the average cost of the Venue in 2019 was $10,500 per event, up from $9,000 in 2018. They also found that October is growing as the most popular month, including in 2020 and that half of all fall weddings are outdoors. This makes a case for rural venue options as being a key factor for those weddings.

The Knot's survey found that the venue is the most significant factor driving costs, with up to 1/3 of the wedding costs being for the venue and nearly 20% of all weddings are at farms, barns, or rural properties.

Also, believe it or not, weddings are still somewhat recession-proof. In 2008, back in the years when the economy was shrinking during the Recession, The National Association of Catering Executives released the membership survey results. This survey found that while couples scaled back their wedding budgets, the total number of cancellations did not rise. I stated in my book in 2016 that unless there was an outright ban on weddings, people are going to be getting married no matter what, and they will still spend money on the location.

Well, in 2020 – there was an outright ban on weddings! And guess what happened? People got married anyway! Sure, some of them broke the law, or they eloped out in the woods with their buddy doing the ceremony or got married in their backyards.

But most couples postponed the event until later in the year or the following year. And some did a mix of both - opting to do a brief, intimate ceremony in 2020 and planned for the whole reception later.

Does that mean more people are going to get married on their properties from now on? Are you kidding? The costs to host your wedding when you don't have the basic furnishings or functionality of an actual venue are high.

So, when weddings return at full scale, they may be smaller in number in terms of overall guests, but I wouldn't worry that everyone will decide that they want to trample their lawn and worry about the chair, table, and linen rentals. No, your business will still be very much in demand.

Another factor to consider for weddings in a post-2020 world is that, sadly, not everyone will survive this, economically speaking. I know this from going through the Recession in 2008. Depending on the venue business structure and whether a family had any other sources of income, some venues and other wedding vendors have been closing their doors entirely or selling to entrepreneurs. I've been approached about buying local rural wedding venues in my area.

And that is because the wedding industry can be ruthless.

No, I don't mean that it's filled with a bunch of cut-throat sharks. I've found it, for the most part, to be quite the opposite. What I do mean is that this industry is very easy to get into. In other words, low barriers to market entry.

So, competition is really high when anyone can jump in and start their business at a relatively low cost. But as a result, people also go out of business very quickly because they don't have the core business skillset to make it. And I don't want that to happen to you.

So, what are we going to cover in this book? A lot. And it can overwhelm you – I promise - especially if you have never started a business before.

Now I don't know your learning style, but I do know that we are all wonderfully different humans. Some people like to go fast and can soak up everything like a sponge. Other people need to go at a slower pace and take time to think about what they heard and learned before moving on. And some are a bit of both.

Because I'm going to go from what seems like zero to advanced learning in one book, I want you to realize that if we were in a classroom, each of these topics could easily be one full hour of class time. And we'd be able to banter back and forth and take the time to process and explain before moving on.

So, to prevent overwhelm, I permit you to read the whole book first without taking any notes or doing any exercise. This way, you can review all the content and see how it all links together. Then go back to the chapters, reread them and start to do the exercises in them, completing each section before moving on to the next. I have found that to be a pretty effective way of limiting the overwhelm factor.

What I wouldn't do is skip around. I have laid these chapters out in order based on my experience as a business coach, entrepreneur, and wedding venue owner. Even if you think you know something already, read the chapter. As someone with experience, I can assume I know everything, but sometimes the chapter isn't about teaching you what you know. Still, often we need reinforcement and a nudge by rereading something practical from someone else for us to take action.

First, I will start with the basics of being an entrepreneur, where I will tell you why businesses fail and how to prevent that. Also, I cover the skills you must have or develop if you don't want to be one of the grim statistics.

I didn't cover this in the first book, but I believe giving people an opportunity to do an honest gut-check is important because not everyone wants to do the self-work involved in self-employment. So, if I'm going to write a book for people who may be starting their first business, I have a responsibility to help you understand some core fundamentals.

Then I will give an *overview of a wedding venue business* to know all that's involved and whether you are the right person or have the right property to do it. Similar to what I spoke to in the original book, I include some 2020 updates.

I also have a chapter not covered in the first book, and this is for people who don't have a property already and want to buy one to start a venue on. And then, I provide a quick primer on land use for anyone finding out that their local jurisdiction (county or city) doesn't allow weddings on rural properties or have never addressed it before in their codes. So, I'm going to give you insights on how policies and codes are written so that if you want to pioneer rural wedding venues in your area, you will know the steps to take to do that.

After that, I go into *market research*, an area of expertise that I help many business owners. I go far deeper than how I cover it in the first book. I expanded it because you will see how important market research is to success as an entrepreneur when I talk about business statistics.

Then I'm going to take you into *branding.* This chapter is excellent, but it is a starter lesson for first-time business owners or people who haven't learned the fundamentals of real branding. However, I promise you that you will have some unique skills after completing it that will help you in any business you ever want to do. In fact, branding is my most popular subject with coaching and other teachings and one of my favorite topics!

After that, we will talk *money* and *basic financial know-how,* and I assure you this won't be like any other business money course you've done. We will talk about your personal financial goals and learn the costs of running a venue. I cover how to determine what to charge, and we're going to make sure that you have a rock-solid foundation to make money doing this by doing some more gut checks on your financial intelligence. This section is also a very popular subject, and I have some advanced learning about this in my other business book for anyone that wants to get even smarter here. But for now, think of this as a beginning to unlearn limiting beliefs about money that will hold you back in business.

As we start to head into the home stretch of the book, I'm going to put you through a couple of chapters about *marketing and sales* and teach you about the Buyer's Journey that we all take when we make a purchasing decision like booking a venue. And I'm going to show you how to design your marketing and website so that you can get a couple to choose you and your venue for their big day.

Then as we wrap up, I will review the *basics of running a wedding venue business*, from putting together a rental agreement to what to expect when you finally host weddings on your property. This section is another carryover from the first book, but I have some updates that will still be worth reviewing. That is because I added some advice on handling our own mistakes without ruining our businesses.

Finally, in the end, I will summarize the book and what I want you to remember most. Plus, I do a chapter on goal setting and planning so that you have some excellent skills to help you as you plot out your adventure in the wedding venue business.

Okay, I'm ready to take another swing at this, so let's get started!

2
BECOMING A BUSINESS OWNER

Before we dive into the details of what a wedding venue business is like and how to start one, I want to begin by talking about entrepreneurship.

Now I'm making a huge assumption that most of you reading this have very little business experience or none at all, and that's okay with me because you all are the very people I love to work with most. I feel this bravery in people who choose to start their own business should be respected and supported. And most of America's small and micro-sized enterprises are created by a person without a business degree or training. All they have is an idea and a lot of guts!

But there is something worth noting that I think many of us have heard, especially when we tell our friends and family that we are going to start our own company and that is a lot of businesses don't make it. For the last several decades, the data has been pretty steady, including recessions, that half of all companies that start in a given year will be closed before they become five years old.

Now, the bright side is that most businesses make it one year. Think of it as the honeymoon period when your enthusiasm is at an all-time high, and your bank account has money in it, and you love everything about being your own boss. You are getting a rush from the small accomplishments you have been making, like having your business card printed with your name on it and the word "Owner" or "President" right underneath. It feels terrific to be in charge.

And then, as the shine starts to wear off and the funds are leaving faster than they are coming in, stress settles in. The work you keep doing over and over again doesn't seem to be paying off as you hoped. The parts of the business you did because you had to now feel like work, and you didn't start your own business just so that you could do stuff you hated, right?

So, you double down on what you love and let the other things slide a little, promising yourself you'll get to it later. Because just like in a marriage, once the honeymoon is over, you realize just how much your partner snores or how often they walk by a dirty kitchen with dishes everywhere and never seem to give you a hand. Or you find out about their addiction to high-end running shoes or anything for sale on Amazon, and you can't seem to save any money for a weekend getaway or couple's massage. And then you wonder if this was a good idea after all.

Weird how half of all marriages end in divorce, just like half of all businesses close.

So, I guess then it's pretty standard for humans to go into significant relationships or situations a bit underprepared, right? It is.

While I wish I could solve the mysteries of human relationships in this book, I think I'll save that puzzle for another day. Instead, I can help you with the business part and how to avoid the pitfalls of entrepreneurship because it doesn't have to be a gamble as to whether or not you end up in the bottom 50% of businesses – the ones who close before five years.

What Is Entrepreneurship

You can find a few definitions and a few debates on whether they are good enough but in simple terms, to be an entrepreneur means that you are starting a business and taking on the risk of doing so. However, the definition falls short of telling you what defines a successful entrepreneur. So, let's investigate that.

In my experience with business and coaching others, anyone needs three essential skillsets to start and run a business successfully. In my opinion, these are the foundation upon which you build your business, no matter what kind of business it is.

Some people may add some other characteristics to this list and argue that they are more critical. These may include traits like passion, grit, resilience, or purpose. And I would agree that those are definitely valuable, and those particular traits alone can certainly make up for what a person lacks in knowledge, experience, or talent. However, I also argue that I have seen plenty of genuinely passionate entrepreneurs fail because they couldn't overcome their incompetence's in the basic skills. Or, as they ran into their weaknesses in those areas, they ignored the problems and hoped that they would overcome them by leaning into their strengths.

But think of it this way: if you are training for a marathon and find that running is hard and you can't seem to go a couple of miles without feeling painfully out of breath, do you stop running? Do you think to yourself, "Well, I really love weight-lifting, so I'll just triple the reps of my squats instead and hope for the best!"

No, of course not. Instead, you realize that running is hard, but if you start slowly and gradually, with patience and practice, you will learn how to do it better, and your body will continue to improve. Or you might decide running sucks, and you don't want to do marathons after all. And that is also a perfectly acceptable answer.

As ridiculous as that example seems, the truth is that in business, some people make very similar choices when it comes to building the skills they need for running their own companies. They validate the reasons to not put too much seriousness in their weaknesses by telling themselves things like, "I'm not trying to run a huge corporation. This business is just a side hustle." Or, "I don't plan on having any employees so that it won't matter in my business."

But the problem is that it does matter. A lot. Because half of all businesses that start in a year are gone before they hit the five-year mark, right? 50-50 sounds like really lousy odds to gamble money and time on, doesn't it? And yet again, that's what a vast majority of people do. They cross their fingers and hope for the best!

So, if entrepreneurs are the people who start businesses and take on the risk of doing it, then successful entrepreneurs know the odds and find ways to beat them. In other words, if starting a business is like doing a marathon, the successful entrepreneur learns how to be a better runner.

Let's look at an analogy I use a lot when it comes to the basic skills of being a business owner: to think of your business as a three-legged stool. All three legs have to be the same length for the stool to be steady and not require much effort to sit on it comfortably. Maybe you can tolerate a little wobbliness if one or two are a bit shorter than the others, but if you're going to sit on that stool for very long, you end up trying to fix it.

Now, if we think of the legs as the skills I'm about to talk about, I want to point out that there is not a perfect overall length of each leg. Your stool can be nice and short, to begin with, and over time, you can increase your knowledge and business acumen, and your stool can get taller and taller. The key is that your stool remains balanced, and you don't spend too much time growing one leg while neglecting the others.

So, the first leg on your stool is **Organization and Planning**. This extensive skillset ranges from having the ability to cross t's and dot i's consistently and sitting down and thinking about long-term goals. The downside of this skill set is that many people possess strength in one but not the other. The particular skills for this leg include:

- Setting goals or deadlines and then coming up with the plan to achieve them
- Being able to set priorities and understand the order to complete work or tasks
- Keeping track of important details or paperwork
- Staying focused while minimizing distractions
- Managing the time chunks you have available and how to use them efficiently to complete your work

Now, organization and planning also include taking a bigger business viewpoint, which is more strategic and creative. These activities include:

- Establishing long-term goals or plans that may take one, two, or even five years to reach
- Consistently reviewing these plans and checking in to see if you are on track
- Being able to predict how long it will take to reach milestones that may be a few months in the future
- Having an ability to study the market and create plans or strategies to adjust as needed
- Being able to develop a variety of different scenarios or outcomes that may happen and predicting potential problems and solutions ahead of time

I have seen many entrepreneurs able to do the long-term visioning parts in the start-up phase of beginning their business, but they forget to check-in and change as needed constantly. I have also seen and met many people who love to dream up the next great adventure but don't spend any time planning out how to get to where they want to because that part is boring or mundane. Or they think the best approach is to dive in and figure it all out along the way.

On the other hand, I have met many entrepreneurs who genuinely love the craft of their business and the work they do or the things they make, that they spend all of their time and energy on that and neglect the planning and management work of their business. And then there are the types of business owners who are very, very good at the detail-oriented work and love the structure of this part of the business but struggle with the less certain, wild unknowns of looking at the future and trying to predict what's next. So, they are happy to keep their heads down and never look up to see if they are going where they want to go.

The next leg or fundamental skillset of entrepreneurship is **Leadership and Interactions with People**. Now, first, I would hope that you are not deciding to go into the wedding venue business with a deep underlying fear of talking to strangers because if you are, well, this could end badly. We'll touch on that more later.

However, I have to point out that this skill set is usually the least developed or, rather, least respected one of the bunch. And maybe "respect" is not quite the right word, but I'm saying that I have met many people running their little businesses who don't like talking about themselves or their business. And so, they don't, and that's a costly mistake. Or they assume that since they don't have any employees, there's no need to put any effort into understanding the finer nuances of leadership and building professional relationships.

Leadership and people skills involve more than just managing others. They include:
- Having the confidence to discuss uncomfortable topics in a constructive manner
- Using influence to have others do what you need, like choose your venue or follow a policy
- Being able to articulate clearly, verbally, and in writing, important details or instructions
- Having an ability to build a connection quickly with someone you've just met and gain their trust

Again, operating a wedding venue business means, by default, you will have a lot of people on your property that you don't know regularly. And it is probably a good idea to know ahead of time if that is something you can handle. But the other facet of self-employment is that even if you are running a one-person business, you regularly engage with customers, other wedding vendors, and suppliers. Therefore, whether you like being around or speaking with people or not, it's an inescapable part of doing business.

This leads us to the worst outcome you can have if you don't prioritize your leadership and people skills. Suppose you aren't convincing or confident about how great your wedding venue business is. In that case, you risk never achieving your sales targets and financial goals, therefore dooming yourself to consistently earning less than you are capable of.

So, now we arrive at the third significant skill set for entrepreneurs, which is **Financial Literacy.** This skill might seem like a no-brainer because if the purpose of a business is to make money and you don't, you will not stay open for very long. But believe it or not, this is by far the trickiest of all the three skills I've covered.

For one, many people have the basic math know-how to do this. However, having full financial literacy is not just knowing how to add and subtract numbers. It also means:

- Paying your bills on time and avoiding late fees and penalties
- Setting budgets and sticking to them
- Being able to forecast things like cash flow and sales
- Understanding how to select the right price for your venue that allows you to meet financial goals
- Having disciplined spending habits

However, the truth is that many people struggle with money and are too ashamed to talk about it. And believe it or not, we carry some ill-fated beliefs about money and wealth into our businesses that will undermine us day in and day out despite our fluency with spreadsheets and checkbooks.

The Main Reasons Businesses Fail

So, after reading about the core skillsets every business owner needs, let's look at why business owners choose to or have to shut down their businesses.

I mentioned earlier that half of all businesses that begin in any given year close within five years. How do I know that? Well, the Small Business Administration's Office of Advocacy tracks business data and, in their 2019 report, found that over the past ten years, the 50% number is pretty steady. Interestingly enough, during the Recession, the business closures did not increase significantly.

I love that stat because it says that when a business owner decides it's time to shut down, it hints that it often has less to do with the actual market and more to do with themselves.

Now I'm going to share one of my favorite bits of business data. CB Insights is a private company that provides market and business intelligence to other companies. And they reviewed over 100 startup post-mortems by former business owners, sifted through the answers, and compiled a list of the top 20 reasons given. I've listed below the top ten with the percentages of how many respondents gave that answer.

1. No market need (42%)
2. Ran out of cash (29%)
3. Not the right team (23%)
4. Got outcompeted (19%)
5. Pricing/Cost Issues (18%)
6. User un-friendly product (17%)
7. Product without a business model (17%)
8. Poor marketing (14%)
9. Ignore customers (14%)
10. Product mistimed (13%)

Okay – now for the fun stuff. Could you see the patterns if I asked you to reorganize this list and put them into three buckets that were the skillsets I just covered? In other words, is it evident that these businesses and their owners might have been a bit weak in one or several of those skillsets?

So, this brings me to the point of this chapter and why I started here before we dove into the specifics of a wedding venue business. Think of this list as the bottom 50% telling you how they got there. And then ask yourself: Do you want to join them? Or do you want to be in the top 50%? I know where I'd like to be.

As a small business coach, I emphasize teaching clients how to remove as many of those reasons on that list as possible. Many of the reasons are generally avoidable, especially for small businesses, if you are willing to learn and apply business-owner-thinking to this venture and not just crossing your fingers and hoping for the best.

Exercise: How Balanced Are You?

Now is a great time to do a bit of self-assessment on your core skills and develop a few ideas for making some improvements. Use the following questions to guide you for each of the three skill sets:

1. Seeing the range of skills involved, how would you rate yourself in each skill set? Are you strong in some areas but weak in others? What are those?

2. Seeing the top ten reasons a business owner shuts down their business, are there any on that list that concerns you? Why? What do you think you could do to prevent it?

3. List out all the resources you might use to strengthen yourself in those areas you identified as weaknesses for you at the moment. Are there online courses you can take? Other books to read? Networking groups with others who are also looking to build similar skills?

3
WHY DO YOU WANT TO START THIS BUSINESS?

I have always been an incredibly imaginative person. As a child, I started to write out all my fantasies in poetry and short stories, and as an adult, I continued to play them out in my head. One fantasy or dream I had when I lived out in the country and in the farming and wedding industry was quitting my day job and doing nothing but work for the farm.

I wanted the tranquility it provided and the creative opportunity to develop a business that would connect people, the planet, and profits. To me, the farm was another re-do of sorts, only this time. It was the chance to resurrect my passion for sustainability.

I drove from the house and passed by the farm property on my way to work in a nearby town. Along the mile-long trip, I imagined a new private driveway that would lead to our new house. I could see the fields filling in with crops for local craft beverage makers like distilleries and breweries. And out in the distance was the free-range chicken coop that I designed and had built with a green roof, reclaimed materials, and nicknamed The Chicken Palace. And every day, as I drove by, I smiled and said to myself, "Someday, this is all you will be doing." And that thought made me happy.

However, to leave the "real world" and make this dream a possibility, I knew that the wedding venue business needed to make sufficient money to pay off my car loan and student loan. The business also had to provide enough income for all basic expenses plus extra savings and travel. I also knew that we had to have stability in revenue and costs and reduce our debt. All in all, to get what I had hoped for required focus and discipline.

This focus helped me endure hard days, but it also helped me know when to high-five myself. See, I had a destination I wanted in my head, and when I successfully took a step in that direction, I could celebrate the progress. And when I had a setback, I just remembered why I was doing all of this and kept going.

My ritual of driving by the farm, seeing all of the details in my head, and feeling all the feelings in my body was like rocket fuel, propelling me along each business decision I made. I knew all of the steps required to get from where I was at that moment and where the businesses were to that future version, and I used that vision to steer everything towards it.

As I mentioned in the introduction, I never realized that dream. And that is okay—more than OK. Of the many lessons that the experience taught me, I saw that some people are naturally geared towards long-range planning, and some are more in the moment and impulsive. And those two kinds of people can make pretty lousy business partners if you ask me.

But let me talk about that a bit because it is important to understand, and it's vital to lay it all out here because it will be a big piece for you and your wedding venue business venture.

When we work without a plan or a vision for where we are going, we may end up making a lot of decisions and choices at the moment that robs us of far more potential than we realize. We say "Yes" more and don't say "No" quite often as we should. We set different priorities or don't set any at all. We just "go with the flow" and accept whatever life throws at us. We are reactive rather than proactive.

Now, don't get me wrong. I'm a pretty laid-back person myself, and I have a mindset that is all about understanding that some things you can control and some things you can't, and the wisdom is in knowing the difference. But do you know what you have a higher degree of control over than you think? Your future.

So, let's ponder the question posed in the title of this chapter: Why do you want to start this business?

Why did I ask that? Well, from various life coaches to financial advisors to manifestation gurus, having a big reason "Why" is the underpinning of your success. It gives you the direction and the destination you are heading towards. It not only helps guide your decisions but, as it was in my case, it helps build your resilience in the face of the adversities and challenges you will face as you develop your own business.

Our "whys" are the emotional center behind the logic of the business itself. Why we are doing our business, whatever it is, is like the eye in the hurricane – it's the safe harbor we come back to time and time again when we need to focus or become re-inspired to keep going.

When some people decide to start a wedding venue business on their property, they may think that "why" they are doing it is because they see a chance to earn extra money. Okay. Cool. That's a good reason. But "why" do you want the extra money? Live debt-free? Travel more? Add on that swimming pool you've been dreaming of so that you can have friends and family over more?

In that example, can you imagine how much more powerful it is to sit and close your eyes and daydream about sitting on the oceanfront deck of your hut in Bali than it is to say you're looking for some extra money?

Now, the other reason it's essential to think of your "why" for this business is when you daydream or use your imagination, and it brings a smile to your face and happy feelings, you are tricking your brain into thinking it's all happening.

Yeah, weird, huh? See, constantly thinking about the future lifestyle you want this business to give you and having your brain and body triggered with the neurochemicals that come with daydreaming makes it feel more natural and possible. And when your brain is thinking, "Man, I think we can do this. I like this," then it's going to help you make better decisions when faced with choices that could keep you from getting to this future you see.

But here's something else about sitting down and plotting out what your future looks like: sometimes you find that you don't need to start your own business to get there. Devoting all your time and money to a business that you have not set up to provide you the financial freedom and resources to grow could prevent you from ever reaching the lifestyle you truly want. It is an insidious form of self-sabotage that many, many people commit. We'll talk about this a little more later.

Finally, aside from keeping you inspired as you do this business, having a more significant reason for why you're taking this on helps you become more flexible when it comes to setting up your business and helps develop a healthy level of skepticism. What I mean is that you are less committed to the exact structure of your business and more to the results. So, if changes are necessary, or you have to pivot, you can think more strategically about re-routing.

So now we're going to go through a series of questions for you to ask yourself before continuing down this path of starting your wedding venue business. The idea is to help tease out some of your more profound thoughts and reasons behind jumping into entrepreneurship. Some of you may know precisely why you're doing this and what life you want. In that case, these will be good reinforcements for you. For those of you in the "I don't know, I just want to earn extra money" or "Because I love being around people" camp, this might push you a bit, and you'll want to reflect on these more deeply before moving forward.

Do not skip these exercises because I will bring us back to your answers several times throughout the book. And as you do them, actually write them down somewhere, either in a journal or notebook or on your computer. Putting these answers into writing makes them real! It takes them from the daydreams in your head and starts to make them look like an actual plan.

Exercise: My Top 20 Goals

Let's start easy. Brainstorm and list out all of the things you would like to experience, achieve, or do in your life and business. Think about your relationships, what you want to do for fun, your financial goals, your health, and so on. Write down at least 20 goals.

Don't think small! And don't stop yourself and come up with why it's crazy or that you can't do it right now. Let that all go and focus on what you want, and don't worry about how you'll get it.

Now, next to each goal, write down the calendar year you hope to achieve that goal. For example, "I will pay off the house by 2030," or "I will have staff running everything in the business by 2022."

Sometimes people do similar exercises, putting in the number of years they will take to reach goals. But I'm a fan of the calendar year approach because it makes the goal more specific and, in my opinion, more realistic. Once you add the calendar year, it's like a clock just started ticking right away. If you put down "Pay off house in ten years," well, when does that ten years start? Two years from now? You could procrastinate on a lot of the work you have to do to make that goal a reality because you didn't give yourself a fixed starting point.

Don't worry if the calendar year you put down is achievable yet. At the end of the book, I will review some tips for goal-setting and planning, and after you've also gone through the rest of the chapters, you'll end up with some skills for figuring out if your wish-list timelines need adjusting or not.

Exercise: How Much Money Do I Want to Make?

Sometimes when I sit down with people to find out what their financial reasons are for starting their own business, they might say, "Oh, I'm not doing this for money. I love weddings and thought this would be a fun business." That is not a terrible answer, but it is the kind of thought process that can trap entrepreneurs into making financial decisions that keep them trapped into under-earning or under-valuing themselves. And, if you circle back a chapter and re-read the reasons businesses had to close, you will find several related to money.

So, before we dive into financials, let's see where you're at right now with your money goals by answering the following questions:
1. Is money a motivating factor for why you want to start your own business? If not, why?

2. Do you want to make more money than you are right now? If so, how much?

3. Are you where you want to be financially now? Is this causing you any pain in your life?

4. If all of your financial needs were met, what difference would this make in your life?

5. If your business made more money than you needed to meet your basic needs and covered all of the business expenses, what would you do with it? Would you grow your business or spend it on doing other things you love?

6. What does financial freedom look like for you? What does that mean?

Exercise: What Is the Ultimate Lifestyle I Want?

Let's bring all this thinking together now at the end and put down in writing what it is you are hoping to achieve with your own wedding venue business. Find a quiet place so that you can limit the distractions outside and in your head, and think about the following questions. Again, write them down and as you read them, close your eyes and feel them in your head and heart. These images and words are your big reason "Why" and are the foundation we will keep building up from throughout this book.

1.   What kind of home or environment are you living in? Describe the details you see and want in your mind.

2.   What does your typical day look like? What are you doing? How are you spending your time? How much is leisure and what are you doing to have fun?

3.   What is your role in your business? Are you working all day or part-time? Are you actually in charge of all decisions, or is it someone else?

4.   What does your perfect work environment look like? Is it a large office in your house? Or do you see your days spent outside as often as possible? Describe the details you see in your mind.

5.   How are you doing financially? Do you have extra money for vacations? Are you donating to causes or organizations you believe in and support? Are you saving it for your children's future? Are you spending it on experiences to share with everyone in your life?

6.   Now, create the perfect lifestyle and the business you love that blends with it – describe what that is.

Exercise: What Is My Big Reason Why?

When you answered the previous questions, did those images make you smile? Did you get a little excited about the possibilities? I hope so! That is the point because once you see it, smell it, taste it, and feel it; you want it. And when you want it, nothing stops you from working towards it.

But why is this lifestyle important to you? What happens if you don't reach these goals? What are you missing out on? That is the final step we have to take – tapping into the core reasons you want to change your life and do something different. So, dig deep and ask yourself the following questions:

1. Why do I want this lifestyle?

2. What is the ultimate goal I'm working towards?

3. What will I receive when I reach this goal that makes me want it so badly?

4. And why do I want that outcome?

After I thought about the direction I wanted my life to go when my adventure in wedding venues ended, I realized that working on a farm for the next twenty or thirty years was not my deepest desire. Knowing myself better now, it could have been disastrous to my mental wellbeing!

Do your reasons why matter? You bet they do! Will your reasons have any influence on your success at this? Definitely, for example, if you are starting this business because it's just to help you make a little extra money, you are apt to try to take all of the short-cuts because you won't think it's worth the time or investment to do something differently.

If, on the other hand, you are choosing to develop a business that can give you the perfect blend of lifestyle and financial freedom, you know that cutting corners is only going to hurt you in the long run and keep you from the life you dream of.

4
SETTING FINANCIAL GOALS

So, before we move into the details of a wedding venue business, I have one last thing to cover with you. And the reason it's so important is that it's the secret behind why 50% of the reasons given for why a business closes were about money.

See, venues often close because after a while of doing it, the business starts to feel like a job that takes all your time and locks you in instead of setting you free. And this happens with a lot of owner/operator type small businesses, where you end up doing all of the work and feel like you have no way of hiring help because you've painted yourself into a corner. That is because our fearless entrepreneurs did not start with clear goals for themselves and their business regarding money.

An often-ignored step is for the owner/operator to set a salary for themselves at day one. In fact, most people figure that they will be paid from whatever is leftover. I hate to tell you, though, that thinking line must stop because you are not the least important person in this business for one. You are the most important! And second, that mode of thinking is a form of self-sabotage that ensures that there will never be anything left over for you later.

Real businesspeople pay themselves a salary. Period. And they don't apologize for it. Ever.

So, if you think your salary is the net profits on the bottom line, it's okay. Sometimes people, especially first-time business owners, start like that because they have no idea what they should be paid for doing this job. And that is because as an owner/operator, you are filling many roles in your venue business on day one, from CEO to the landscaper, which makes it confusing.

Plus, if you ask other venue owners what they are making, the odds are they are working off the "whatever is leftover" mode, and they probably don't know how much that ends up being at the end of the year. So, let's poke around at a few numbers to get a rough idea.

Finally, many business owners will tell you that you can't make what you want right away as you're starting your business, which is true. But a savvy business owner has a plan and clear targets to know what and when they will pay themselves.

Now, even though you are picking weeds and cleaning toilets, and other days you are sitting in an office doing marketing, I want you to realize all of it is business management when you are self-employed. No, it's not all glamorous, but you are the boss, and there is no business without you. And if you want to know what other people have the responsibility to manage enterprises to make, you can find out by checking out the Current Population Survey (CPS) done by the U.S. Census Bureau.

In their 2019 survey results, women in "Management Occupations" had a median income of $1,266 per week or $65,832 per year. "Median" is not the same as average. Instead, it means 50% of the women surveyed made less than that, and 50% made more. On the other hand, men in the same 2019 survey had a median income of $1,659 per week or $86,268 per year.

In fact, according to the statistics, women's median salaries were about 60-81% of men's salaries for the same positions. If you want to get into that discussion with me, I'd be happy to do it, but it's not in this book. However, I want to point this out for my female readers because it demonstrates a potential pitfall you can run into if you go out and survey your other female friends to find out what they are making. The odds are that they will give you a lower number than if you interviewed your male friends. And if you set a salary based only on comparing yourself to other women, you are highly likely picking a number that is lower than it should be. So, aim high.

But another thought here before you pick your number and move on: if you will put the time and energy into this venue business of yours, think hard about making it so that you can take care of yourself and your family if you need to, on your own. Because you never know if this business will be the only income you have.

Setting Your Lifestyle Levels

So back to your salary. Knowing the salary ranges from the CPS data, what wage will give you the lifestyle you want? To figure this out, I want to share with you an exercise I use. Let's think of your financial goals as four levels of a video game, called your Lifestyle Levels. Level 1 is where you begin, and Level 4 means you beat the game. So, open a spreadsheet on your computer, get all your bank records together and figure these out.

Level 1: What do you need to make to be financially secure? This is the amount of money you must make to have your basic needs met and peace of mind, and you didn't have any other income coming in. In other words, this is the lowest amount you need to earn.

Level 2: What do you want to make to be able to upgrade your life? This is the income level that covers all your expenses plus some extra. Now, at this level, you will have to define what "upgrades" are to you. It could be money for more exotic vacations, adding on that pool, or paying off all your debts early. Make that list and add it to your expenses and see what you end up with.

Level 3: At what point are you making enough money to be financially separate from working at all? This level means you are creating enough passive or residual income with your business that you don't need to be involved on a day-to-day basis because you have employees taking care of the work. Now, to achieve this level faster, you might aim for your Level 1 income and give up on some of the upgrades. That's up to you.

Level 4: How much money gives you financial power and ultimate freedom? This is the mega level – the final level of the game. In other words, how much money does it take for your business to earn so that you don't have to work at all, and you can have everything you ever dreamed of.

We will use these numbers in a later chapter when I show you how to figure out how much to charge for your venue. But right now, we are still on a little bit of a psychology journey, so bear with me.

After sitting down and figuring out the numbers for the four levels, ask yourself the following questions to help you understand your mindset about wealth and financial freedoms.

- How do these numbers look? Am I excited about making this much money?
- Do some of the numbers seem lower than I'd thought? Higher?

- How does it make me think about setting up my venue business to achieve all four levels? Or am I happy with Level 1 or Level 2?
- Do I believe that any of this is possible? Why or why not?
- If I want to level up, what are my timelines for when that happens?
- Does my partner/spouse believe any of this is possible too? Are we both on the same page regarding the financial goals and reasons for doing this venue business?

That last one –important. Really important. Trust me. If you and your partner have vastly different reasons or ideas about handling money, the business will not make it. Period. So, before you start investing heavily in buying a new property or improving your existing property, make sure you are both on the same page.

You both must want to achieve the same Level, believe you can, and agree on how to do it. If not, you will struggle to make good decisions together. Or worse, your partner could end up undermining your efforts.

So, I recommend that you have a conversation, many times if need be, about these goals. If you never agree and don't have the freedom to pursue and run this business all on your own, don't start this at all. Please.

What Are Your Money Mindsets?

So now that I drove home the fact that we have to think about paying ourselves in our businesses and that too many people never do, I want to give you some hints on why that happens.

It's not about math. Instead, it comes down to our feelings about money in our culture and probably what our families believed. And I want to bring this up for you now, early in the book, because later, when I show you how to set your pricing, I hope you can see how tiny tweaks to your thinking can have substantial financial benefits to you.

So, this is another topic that if you have some wiggles in your gut while we talk about this, I highly recommend you get curious and explore that more before you dismiss them and run into starting a business. Or else you'll be in the bottom 50% with the other businesses who all said they had money problems. Maybe not in year one, but sooner or later, it will catch up to you. So, let's look at the following questions:

- How does it feel when the bills come in the mail every month?

- How does it feel when you have asked for a raise or to be paid for your work?
- How do you feel when you are around wealthy people?
- How do you feel about the financial aspects of your business?

I'd like you to think about each of those questions, and I invite you to grab a journal and write down your thoughts. Why? Because I want to raise your awareness that you have them and get you to start thinking about why you have them.

Okay, let's swing back to the Lifestyle Levels numbers and think about these questions you answered. Do you believe it's possible to create a venue business capable of achieving those different levels for yourself? If not, really ask yourself why you think that. And if your negative feelings about money are uncomfortable, I recommend you keep doing some additional work on what is behind them. And I have other resources available for that at the end of this book.

In the end, as we bring this back full-circle, having a great or unique idea in business is not enough. Great ideas die all the time, in fact, about 50% of the time. The key to making money as an entrepreneur will be to make sure you are on top of the psychology of it all. I preach this everywhere, but I have seen this for myself in the venue business world. Great venues struggle because of impulsive, wasteful spending, underpricing, not realizing it, or being too afraid to change.

And so, if your head is messing with you right now a little, then before we continue through this book, I want to give you some tips for dealing with those negative thoughts.

Hang out with people who like making money. One of the big keys to overcoming our negative beliefs about money is to start looking for proof that none of those beliefs are true. And usually, the best way to do that is to hang with people who don't have negative money beliefs themselves, like these:

- There isn't enough money
- This industry just doesn't pay well
- Money isn't as important as hard work/purpose/etc.
- Money is evil and wealthy people are corrupt

See, we tend to hang out with people who all sort of share the same beliefs around what's normal about money and how much we should be making. And you might notice that if you make any attempts to rise above that or to do and think differently, you get blowback from everyone else around you. So then, you think you're wrong, and your friends and family are right – and you stay where you are. I have seen this also within the wedding community itself, other venue owners who think you're crazy for charging what you do and telling you that "no one is going to pay you that to get married at your place."

But in the venue business, your network also includes your customers or couples. One of the hardest things I help business owners break up with their customers who loved that the venue was undercharging. It was the first I did with my venue when I took over, and I've done the same with others since. And it starts by setting up a business and marketing plan to help attract new couples willing to pay what the venue is worth.

And I've also done this with other wedding vendors who were undercharging, like photographers and DJs. It's scary to think about breaking up with your "bad" customers, especially if they are nice people, but it must be done. There is always push back from those who want the lower price. And, even for a little while, you may see a dip in the sales. But as you focus your marketing on the right paying couple, the sales will rebound. Trust me.

Stop lying to yourself. First, we all do it. We all have these little excuses we make for why we keep doing something the same way. But the problem is those lies are the very things that keep us making the same mistakes or choices that get in our way. And the lies around money – well, those can leave us underearning until we catch ourselves doing it and stop.

So how do we overcome the lies we've been telling ourselves as it relates to money and business? Well, we give you a different mantra to focus on based on the truth. So here are a few common lies and truths as examples, but you should see if you can think of more.

LIE: "I can't pay myself because my business won't be as profitable."
TRUTH: "I realize that there is no business without me. It's my company. And I started it so that I could be financially free, not so that I could be an employer and pay other people what I should/could be earning myself. I'm running a business, not a charity!"

LIE: "Doing something I enjoy is more important than making money."
TRUTH: "Doing something I enjoy and making money are not mutually exclusive of each other. In fact, I'm grateful that I can do both so that I have

the financial resources to do more of what I love and not have to sacrifice my financial wellbeing to do work I'm passionate about!"

LIE: "No one is willing to pay that high of prices."
TRUTH: "I have done a lot of research and have found evidence from other venues like mine that I can sell my venue at a price that provides me with the financial resources I need to live my life the way I want. I simply need to adjust my marketing and the customers I'm targeting, but I know they are out there and what I do is worth those prices too."

Always Come Back to Your Big Reason Why. The research and practical experience from the professionals in financial planning all agree that people who focus on their goals and plans, particularly the lifestyle they want to be living, instead of dollars and cents, all do better at sticking to their plans.

One of the financial experts I work with, Dr. Brad Klontz, who wrote a great book called Mind Over Money, did his study with people in five different states and found the exact same things.

In his study, they had two groups of participants. One group was put into a financial literacy class and taught saving money and setting budgets. Another group was told instead to visualize and get excited about what they were saving for. They were told to focus what the benefits were to them, like a vacation or new home. Then this group created vision boards and wasn't given any financial literacy training at all.

The savings rate of the financial literacy group grew by 20%, which is great. But the group that got excited about their big reason "Why" increased their savings rate by 70%! Why? Because they could see that not saving money was only keeping them from getting the future they really wanted.

When people shift away from just focusing on how much money they made and being driven to live their best lives they feel they deserved, surprisingly, people start making more money.

So, as you fight your inner war, remember what you are fighting for: yourself. Your dreams. A life that you deserve to have for yourself and your family. And I want to make sure as you design this venue business for yourself to do just that. Otherwise, you are robbing yourself.

5
THE WEDDING VENUE BUSINESS OVERVIEW

Alright, finally, we are at the wedding venue business stuff. I hope you can appreciate why we've covered the basic skills entrepreneurs need and the typical reasons half of all businesses end up closing in less than five years. And I also hope you have gotten some benefit from doing an exercise in setting your personal goals for how much money you want to earn from this business. After all that, now we're ready to get into learning more about starting and running a wedding venue business.

The Venue Features

You might be on this path to becoming a wedding venue owner because you went to a wedding at someone's private property or farm and thought to yourself, "Hey, we could do this at our place." And the truth is, you probably can.

So, assuming you didn't get a really good look at the entire operation while you were there, let me outline the basics required for a wedding and event location that will have maximum appeal. As I'll speak to you later, you can have different variations of everything I walk you through. But if you want to make serious money in the summer, you need to be minimally competitive with what most venues offer.

Changing Rooms. Your venue should provide two spaces or large rooms for both people getting married. The old-school mentality that it's all about the Bride does not work these days. Most couples today are partners and have grown up in a culture of equality. But, even as important is the fact that after the Supreme Court's historic decision in 2015, legalizing same-sex marriages, you will find that sometimes there isn't even going to be a bride or groom at one of your events! That means make them awesome and beautiful but keep them Gender Neutral.

The rooms or areas should be big enough to accommodate a groom or bride and several of the wedding party members. There also needs to be areas to sit and relax, places to hang clothing, and several mirrors. And how big are wedding parties these days? Studies show that many couples have ten of their closest friends and family members standing at the altar with them. So, these rooms have to safely fit about eight people each. That means a room about the size of a double-occupancy hotel room.

Okay – what if you don't have that? I know many venues with smaller changing spaces (like a small bedroom), and they are considered "holding" rooms for the couple before the ceremony. And the expectation is that the full preparations are done offsite if you have a big wedding party. But if it's a small affair, they work out nicely.

Also, a lot of photography happens in this room. That's why making the rooms attractive is important because they are mini photo studios. So, think about areas in the changing rooms that would make good places for pictures. And think about where the photographer would stand to capture those memories. And if you don't know how exactly to do that, ask for help from a local wedding photographer. They'd love to give you some tips because people hardly ever ask how to set up a space that makes it easier for them to do their jobs.

Now, not a requirement, but a nice bonus would be an alternate third, probably smaller space for non-wedding party family members or the wedding planner. I've often seen these folks in need of a place to change their work clothes after decorating the venue all day but end up doing it in a bathroom stall. For this, think dressing rooms in a store –a few private niches in one space with privacy curtains, where there is a clean place to sit, and it's not a toilet.

Catering Prep Area. This does not need to be a full kitchen for a top-of-the-line destination, rural or farm venue. In fact, if you want to keep your life simple, do not ever put in a full kitchen as this may introduce some additional permitting and regulations. All you need is a room or area with access to hot water for hand-washing, somewhere to bring in food, plate it, clean up dishes, and not do it in front of the guests. It also helps if the caterer can drive up close to the area to load and unload.

Some venues can get away with a large tent, while others, like my venues, had a separate space in a building on the property. Some have refrigeration provided. Others do not. I've spoken to many caterers who have worked at weddings at rural properties over the years, who don't have any areas specifically for them at all, leaving them to work under a pop-up tent or inside a cramped catering truck.

My tip here is maybe you can't have the Catering Prep area in your venue plans the first year, and that's okay but think about adding it soon. Caterers are great influencers with couples and, if a caterer has an easy time working at your place, they are more apt to recommend it.

A Ceremony Location. This should be a large, wide, open area with terrain suitable for guests to sit on chairs or benches and see the couple and officiant. Some people locate the Ceremony site on the property where there are some exceptional views or vistas for the background. Others freshen up barns or outbuildings, offering a truly rustic setting that can serve as a backup in case of inclement weather. Access to the Ceremony site should be easy for people with limited mobility or need wheelchairs or other assistive devices. This means no steep, rocky hikes to get to it. Making sure Grandma, who is in a wheelchair, can easily get to the front row for the ceremony is a pretty important consideration for a couple when choosing a venue.

A Reception Area. Ideally, this is another large area that should be set up for the reception, which is the dinner and party portion of the event and is separate from the Ceremony site. There should be spaces within this area for dinner tables and chairs and a flat, level area for a dance floor. This location also includes suitable space for catering buffet tables, a place for the Bar, and be near the restrooms. Electrical outlets are also necessary here for the DJ and decorative lighting.

Restrooms. This requirement speaks for itself, but generally not understood is how many you'll need. While local codes may vary and your planning department or architect will help tell you exactly, a rule of thumb is that you need one toilet for every 125 men and another for every 100 women.

So, if you are planning on creating a large capacity venue, you may find you will need up to four restrooms. Some jurisdictions might allow you to provide temporary restrooms for just the season, while others will make you build permanent facilities, which could require an upgrade to a septic system if you have one. These days, "temporary" doesn't necessarily mean "porta-potties," which not many couples like, but they're used at many rural venues. You can rent out portable toilet trailers for a season. These are spacious, ADA-accessible, and attractive enough on the outside to not undermine the ambiance of your beautiful property.

Parking. Your local codes might dictate otherwise, but another rule of thumb is four people per car. So, taking your Venue's capacity, determine how many cars you will need parking for – and then add some extra for the vendors working the event and overflow.

In my experience, if you can accommodate a parking rate calculated based on two people per car, you should have plenty. In this area, make sure you have ADA parking spots close to the main parts of the venue.

So, parking for 250 guests takes up a good 3/4 to 1 acre of land. Parking does not mean it has to be paved. Some rural or farm venues actually have parking on grass, which looks nice and is relatively easy to maintain.

And other jurisdictions might allow you to use permeable pavers – which can be planted with grass to look more natural and allow water to percolate through them but are sturdy enough to provide a firm area for traffic.

Storage. If you decided to purchase a large tent to provide shade or backup rain protection, it needs to go somewhere in the off-season. Additionally, if you supply tables and chairs, those need an off-season storage area to keep them from getting damaged or dirty. But minimally, you're going to need an area to keep your lawn tools, mowers, rakes, trash bags, trash cans, and all of the stuff you don't want lying around while people are on the property. Plan on a storage area about the size of a 1 or 2 car garage.

High-Speed Internet. Now, back before 2020, having high-speed internet access at a rural property wasn't a necessity. One of my venues didn't have it at all, and it was fine. Today, however, I believe all rural venues should strongly consider bringing high-speed access and offering Wi-Fi and streaming options for their weddings. For one, it is uncertain how long the coronavirus impacts will continue to linger and put certain populations at risk, such as Grandma and Grandpa or your friend who's been bravely fighting cancer.

But what I think will permanently change in the wedding industry is the result of how well everyone learned and adapted to how to interact with each other virtually, which may impact wedding guest lists from now on. No, not everyone will give up on traveling for weddings, but if you are a venue that offers a couple the ability to stream their event to their out-of-town friends and family – you will definitely have a service that will be in demand.

This is a great feature for guests who may be too ill to travel and for families with small children. Live event streaming is also an option for those who can't afford the costs of an airplane ticket and hotel to see their old friend or distant cousin tie the knot.

And I think it will be a huge benefit for couples who now won't feel pressured to have large guest lists and can have smaller, more affordable affairs yet still have the option for others to join them digitally – which wasn't even a thought in anyone's mind before 2020.

You can see from the list above that various areas are required to become a full-service wedding and event venue. So, what sized property can accommodate all those zones and facilities? Well, you would need at least 1 acre for a venue that can accommodate 100 people or a minimum of 2 to 3 acres for larger, 250-person weddings.

And what if you don't have these ideal minimum requirements? Does this mean you give up? No. I'm all about creative thinking, and there are solutions to everything. And I believe if you have a real desire to earn extra income off your rural property or farm by hosting weddings and events, there is a way. Here are some alternate options.

Ceremony Only. You can just be (or start as) a great-looking place for the ceremony only. This works well if you have something spectacular or unique such as a private, wooded area with a secret clearing in the center or has a stunning view of the mountains. If you have the picturesque landscape features that will look great in wedding photos, there is a market for you out there. Your couples and families can get ready someplace else and then, afterward, travel to the reception location at another spot – it's been happening this way since people have been getting married in churches.

This could be great for smaller locations, and you could even advertise it as an elopement option. In 2020, with smaller gatherings happenings, the small venues I knew had a regular business doing elopements and micro weddings that were ceremonies only.

Shared Ceremony and Reception Area. This requires good planning with seating and tables ahead of time and ensuring you have the space to put all of the guests while the room is "flipped" from the ceremony set-up to the reception set-up.

If there isn't any overflow for a cocktail hour during the room flip, you can set the space up for the reception and have the guests sit at the tables during the ceremony. I've seen that done many times. So, look at your property and see some creative ways to combine both functions into one area.

Reception Only. While I never had a couple rent us for just the ceremony, we did get a fair number of couples who rented us only for the reception. These couples usually have their ceremonies at churches, mosques, or temples because of their religious traditions. Or they had a private ceremony with only close friends and family in attendance and saved the big party for later. So, if you choose to be a reception site only, you don't need changing rooms, which can be helpful if you have a smaller site with few existing buildings to work with.

Again, these are the basics for a venue with some variations sprinkled in there. And I want you to realize that, honestly, there isn't a true magic formula for how to convert a rural property into a revenue-earning wedding venue. If you are creative and persistent, any property can be marketed well to gather your customers who want what you have.

The Venue Capacity

Another part of operating a wedding venue is deciding how big the weddings you want to provide a space for. So let's talk about those quickly because what you decide will be based partly property size, how much of your property you want to convert into the venue, and how much you want to keep for yourself.

The Value of Being Small - Up to 100 People. If you don't have a lot of space to put in all of the venue areas listed above, you might have to establish your venue as a specialty, smaller location and focus on groups of up to 50-100 people.

When couples are massaging their wedding budget numbers, the largest lever they have in managing their expenses is the catering, which ties back to the size of their guest list. So, many couples might go for fewer people, but they still want superior, more personalized services and a beautiful, unique location.

There are some great venues out there that are small, garden-style locations. And others are very small farms that use a barn for a ceremony or reception space while using portions of the farmhouse for changing rooms. And these venues can get great lease rates because the emphasis is on a beautiful, intimate setting rather than just a big space. And with gathering restrictions implemented in 2020, the demand for smaller venues increased, not just because of the size. Still, the smaller locations are typically more affordable than larger venues.

The Value of Being a Big Venue – Up to 250-300 People. Many weddings are larger affairs, in the range of 125-250, with the average size being around 140. So, overall, the demand is high for more extensive spaces in the market, which is why people seek out rural properties or locations for their events. Therefore, the best money and value are in a big venue if you can handle the larger groups.

The Value of Being Both. When thoughtfully planned and thought out, your venue can be designed to work well for both small and large weddings. Small wedding parties are worried that their group will feel overwhelmed in a large space like a barn or a hotel banquet room. So, if you are a venue with large spaces, it's advantageous to know how to help a smaller wedding understand how you can set up the barn for them so that they don't feel like the space is out of proportion to their numbers.

In 2020, this was a huge pivot for venues when stay-at-home orders and "safe start" plans went into effect, eliminating large gatherings of over 50 people for a while. The venues that could take a large location and make it more intimate for smaller weddings fared better than those who didn't. And so, I think the trend for wedding venue owners moving forward is how to do both.

Here's another tip from me: again, if creativity is not your strong suit, then reach out to some local wedding planners who provide design and decorative services and invite them to your space to brainstorm ideas.

The Seasons

Now, let's review how a wedding season is determined and what the workload looks like year-round.

So, as you create your venue business plan, you want to decide when your venue is open for business to host weddings. And this decision is based on what is considered **wedding season** in your area. You also need to consider how much of your year you want to have your property on loan to a few thousand people.

The most popular month for weddings can vary yearly, but most wedding professionals consider June through September the true wedding season.

And this was based largely on school schedules and summer vacations. But the latest research on trends shows October has jumped up to the highest month for weddings in the US. I also mentioned earlier that 50% of the weddings in the fall being outdoor events. And so, if you are planning on being an outdoor event space, you'll still capture the highest volume of possible bookings by only operating in the summer to early fall.

For your first forays into this business, I always recommend starting simple and not over-extending yourself before you have a handle on all the work involved. Also, it's important to get an idea of how your property will hold up under constant wear and tear. Many people have no idea that your lovely little lawn may not be able to handle the foot traffic weddings bring. And you don't want to watch your beautiful property degrade from green to dirt before you've finished hosting weddings for the season.

So, in year one, think about doing it for a 3-month time frame. And then, after that, you could consider tagging on a month in the spring or the fall, depending on your location. But, again, I recommend you do that only after you have a grasp on the maintenance required for the property and you feel like you can handle the extra effort that comes with booking, servicing, and coordinating the events.

Let me say this again too – doing weddings is hard work. I had a stretch in the summer of 2017 of (9) weeks in a row working a wedding every Friday, Saturday, and Sunday PLUS the open houses on Wednesday, rehearsals on Thursdays, and ladies and gentlemen – my regular day job as a business coach. And I'm not done yet: Mom to two teenagers!

Later, we will talk more about sales targets, and we've already covered lifestyle goals. But picking your season also involves deciding whether you want to work your butt off 9 to 12 weekends in a row. I think you can imagine why many wedding venue business owners/operators burn out because they get too ambitious, and they didn't do the thoughtful planning I'm teaching you.

If your venue is all outdoors, obviously, the weather will ultimately dictate your exact season. For example, in the Pacific Northwest, where my venues were, booking weddings in May for outdoor venues is a terrible idea unless you supply raincoats and umbrellas. Some even argue that June is dicey. I nicknamed June the "white knuckle month" because it could either be amazing or soggy. So, in the coastal Pacific Northwest, the best months are July through September.

Now, when you look at other areas around the country, like Arizona, summer is too hot for outdoor venues, so the peak seasons may be Spring (April & May) and then back again in the Fall (September & October). If you have coverage or structures, such as a barn or old horse arena, the weather may have little impact on the location, especially if there is heating or air-conditioning. Because of these differences, I recommend you research your location to determine your region's typical.

Hopefully before we wrap this section up, you realize that a wedding venue business is a year-round operation. True, the services you provide might only be 3-4 total months out of the year but renting your property out for weddings and events has a lot of other work involved.

For example, most people don't realize one aspect of the wedding industry is that there is an engagement season. It's the time of the year, starting around Thanksgiving and ending soon after Valentine's Day, because couples tend to get engaged and then share the big news with their families during the holidays. Over 30% of all engagements happen in the same, two-month period, and most occur in December.

This means for venues that typically right after the New Year, the hunt for the date and location begins! It also means that during Engagement season, bookings can decline, and your cash flow will slow. But overall, doing tours and booking couples happens throughout the year, so that means while work activities change, there isn't ever an off-season with a venue business. So, in addition to constant marketing and sales, keeping the venue clean and looking good is also a year-round activity.

The People

Finally, let's talk briefly about the staffing it takes to operate a venue business and a bit about the work they do. In my experience, with a basic venue operation, four major roles need to be fulfilled. In the early days of your business, most of them can certainly be handled by just you and maybe one other person. And, if you choose to keep working and be involved with everything, you can keep doing so.

But if your Lifestyle Levels include Level 3 and even Level 4, then at some point, you have to find other people to sit in these positions and handle the work for you so that you can be paid but not be tied to the day-to-day. That's why, as you see on this list, you should also consider how much it's going to cost to hire a person to replace you, either fully or partially, and carry that over into the chapter later when we discuss pricing.

Overall, some of these roles can be combined into one person, assuming that this one person can fulfill all of the responsibilities.

A Great Business Manager. This is a well-rounded person who is capable of the three core skills I mentioned in Chapter 2. This role might be you, and if your plans involve a Level 3 lifestyle goal, you'll eventually hire someone to replace you. In either case, a successful wedding venue business manager can do the following:

- Manage and schedule tours, weddings, and other important appointments
- Coordinate and hire any extra help such as repair people, landscaping, and housekeeping
- Coordinate and manage all activities related to ongoing work on the property and be prepared on time for the wedding season to begin
- Keep track of all venue contracts, payments received, money still to be collected, and make sure to not double-book weddings
- Provide timely and friendly help and support to couples with their wedding planning questions through phone, email, and in-person
- Make sure the business is current on business licenses, insurance, and permits
- Perform basic bookkeeping tasks such as collecting income, developing budgets, forecasting expenses, and paying bills on time

Now let me kick the money horse a little more. There is a lot of money to be earned in this business. However, you will not profit from this business if you don't know how to keep it. A venue business owner who starts getting big checks in (and trust me – there are BIG checks in this business) but starts spending the money without care for a budget or planning will find themselves in a dangerous situation. For one, if your wedding cancels and you are asked to return their deposits or payments, you are now in a negative cash flow situation. We'll talk about that more later.

But also, if you don't have the money available to buy all of the things you need to put on the event months later because you spent it all on upgrades you didn't need or blew it on a new car, you are going to tank your business and reputation very quickly.

See, collecting $20,000 in one weekend after doing tours and booking weddings is very intoxicating. Trust me. I've done that many times with my venue businesses. Once you're up and going, that kind of money is to be expected. But that's a lot of cash in hand; many people are not used to holding that much. The first time you're staring at all those checks on the kitchen counter, it's a little like feeling you won the lottery. And you all have heard about lottery winners who go broke fast, right?

The truth is that a wedding venue often goes out of business due to how they handle money and not being disciplined.

A Marketing and Sales Team. This is another role that, at the onset, you may be doing as well as overall management. However, when you compare the overall time and efforts of the Business Manger to the Marketing & Sales position, there is far more work involved in this position regularly than the other, so hopefully, you have some real marketing strengths and know-how. If not, your sales will suffer. This work includes:

- Maintain a constant online presence on Social Media
- Create marketing materials like flyers, business cards, and social media graphics
- Host tours & Open Houses with prospective couples
- Attend and represent your business at networking events
- Represent the venue at trade shows and other similar events
- Maintain relationships with those who provide word-of-mouth or referral business for you, such as wedding vendors, local restaurants, the Chamber of Commerce, etc.
- Create blog content for the website

A Maintenance and Repair Team. This function is almost really two different types of people. Still, all these activities can be done by one person who enjoys the physical labors of running a wedding venue business and ensuring the property is in good condition for weddings and tours. And I know a lot of people who prefer a hands-on type of job like this.

First, the role is a Handy-Person for basic maintenance and repairs. Suppose you are that person – awesome. This role involves keeping toilets running, fixing holes in the wall, and even repairing a broken table or chair. But this person is also helpful for cleaning up the property the morning of an event to get it ready for the next wedding, taking the garbage and recycling out, and being ready and available in case of an emergency to repair or fix something mid-wedding. And those things do happen!

In the off-season, this person's responsibilities shift to touching up paint, light remodeling, winterizing restrooms, storing away equipment and furnishings used during weddings, and other activities like that.

An outdoor wedding venue also requires a Landscaper to keep the property looking good and healthy year-round. The work is just about maintenance in the off-season, like keeping the leaves raked up and the pathways free of snow or ice. But in the heat of the wedding season, you, or someone you hire, will be doing work weekly to prep the property before the weekends. This includes wedding flowerbeds, mowing the grass to perk it up, or repairing lawn areas that might have gotten trampled or damaged.

A Chaperone or Venue Host is a seasonal position or role for just the weddings themselves. While some people don't have this position, I strongly believe it's good business to have a chaperone, and I have played this part many times. If this is you initially, then as your business grows and you decide you don't want to spend an entire weekend playing host to your wedding business, you can hire out this position. I often used local wedding planners who have the day off and want to earn a few bucks. We also used a staff member at times to do it. On busy weekends during wedding season, it could easily be (3) 12-hour days in a row plus rehearsals, so that's a legitimate full-time position. It might be a great role for a student or teacher who has the summer available to work.

The primary functions of the chaperone are to make sure the guests and couple are happy and safe and to ensure the property is undamaged at the end of the event. Ensuring both of those things happen is why I recommend having this position. Now, if you are not going to stay on-site during the whole event because it's too costly to pay someone and meet your financial goals, it's very important to have procedures in place to contact you in an emergency. You also want to have a process in place to know where to get extra supplies such as toilet paper, trash bags, or hand soap if they run out during the wedding. And you would certainly want to make sure that at the end of the event, you or the chaperone is on hand to oversee the clean-up and break-down to make sure it's done properly.

Now, it's a bonus if your chaperone is also a handy person, as was in my case. With all my experience in engineering and construction, I could fix most plumbing, furniture, and electrical issues with a smile on my face and keep the party going.

Sure, you could call a local plumber's 24-hour emergency number when your toilets get clogged during a wedding, but you'd be flushing profit right down the drain. There are occasions – like remodels or massive repairs (broken water mains, for example) – when you have no choice but to call in the professionals. However, it pays to have someone on the property who knows how to get things fixed for most contingencies.

In the end, it doesn't take much more than these positions to run a wedding venue, which is what makes this type of business so attractive. Labor is a very expensive cost of doing business. So if you have a company with a structure that doesn't require a lot of different people to keep it running, then it gives you more flexibility, and it helps to keep your costs pretty controlled and as low as possible.

6

WEDDING VENUES AND LAND USE POLICY

Okay – big section here with the million-dollar question: Can you do weddings on your property? Now, some people bought my original version of this book because they wanted me to answer that question for you and were disappointed that I didn't just come right out and say yes or no. But I will say this again in this version of the book; I can show you how to figure that out independently because it's not a straightforward process, as I will explain.

After I published the book, I also coached several would-be venue owners who were in situations where the codes were not very clear because the county or township hadn't had to figure out how to allow for this type of activity to take place rural properties. So, that's why I have a section that gives an overview of how municipalities create policies and codes.

Not many people know that years before I was a wedding venue owner, I was a private building consultant for a Seattle suburb. As a member of the Major Development Review Team, my role was to work with large commercial and residential builders and developers on land use regulations and apply sustainable building practices. I came about that position not only because of my experience in construction but I also have a master's degree in Environment & Community, with my practicum being "Sustainable Policy Development." So, this is an area I know about being a business owner and being on the other side of the coin.

This brings us to you, your property, and how to answer the million-dollar question. Well, the first step is to go online and look up your local codes and see if wedding businesses are allowed on rural or agricultural properties. No, it doesn't matter if you know other people already doing it. The truth is, they may not be doing it legally. And as your quasi-personal consultant here, I want to make sure you realize your priority in starting this business is to make sure it's legal! And so, I'm not teaching you how to be the kind of people who take shortcuts that put their businesses in jeopardy.

I can't just have a simple yes or no answer to the big question because different counties and municipalities have different rules for what kind of home-based businesses can be conducted on properties. However, people who don't know how these codes work make a lot of assumptions, and one of them is that when you live way out in the country, it doesn't matter what you do on your property. Unfortunately, when one considers the probable impact to the neighborhood (no matter how rural), as well as the concerns for the health and safety of wedding guests, you can't assume you can simply start your venue business without concern for codes. That's why you have to go online and see where you stand.

If you're not much for online research or if your municipality doesn't have all the codes and ordinances online, then the easy thing to do is to set up a meeting with a Building Department Specialist or Planner. Suppose they tell you that wedding facilities are allowed on your property. In that case, they will also give you a run-down of the procedures you will need to implement to secure the proper licensing or permits for the business.

Meeting with a Planner

Before this meeting, I suggest you have a basic property diagram ready for your meeting to better explain your intentions to the Planner. Your diagram doesn't have to be drafted by a professional. If you can sketch out a clear picture, get a ruler and a big sheet of paper and do it by hand. Here's a guide to help you prepare your diagram and Venue Plan.

First, I recommend using an online tool such as Google Maps to get an aerial view of your property. The County or City already have this on file, but they likely won't bring it to your meeting, so be proactive and provide it.

On this diagram, denote all property line dimensions. This is important if there are any "setback" issues with certain features of the property. Setbacks are various rules to ensure everyone is neighborly by not putting noisy activities or buildings next to the adjacent properties or protected natural areas.

Also show all existing buildings, indicating which ones are for weddings and which aren't. And have the sizes of the buildings and pictures for the Building/Planning Department person to see.

On this diagram, you also want to mark off the wedding-related areas, such as your Parking lot, Ceremony location, Reception area, restrooms, etc. This is so you can be ready to discuss the following:

- ADA Accessibility includes parking spaces, walkways, ramps into buildings, and hardware and sizing of the restrooms.
- Traffic, such as how many vehicle trips are expected and what time of day, plus making sure the approach road to your property is wide enough for emergency vehicles to pass around cars.
- Your property's drinking water source and the sewage/waste system.
- Electrical service to the property and the location of any existing or new electrical outlets or panels
- Life safety includes exits and clear exit routes inside and outside buildings, fire lanes and access, smoke detectors, fire hydrants, fire extinguishers, etc. For this line item, it's helpful to know that building codes require at least two exits for spaces or rooms with more than 50 people.

In addition to this diagram, bring your operational information to your meeting like how big weddings you are trying to host. Are you wanting to do both ceremonies and receptions (with caterers bringing in food?) And how many months are you open for weddings?

Also, you may end up needing to speak with the Fire Marshal if you are going to convert a barn into a part of your wedding venue. Based on the size and number of stories in the barn, the number of people you want to have in it, and your water sources on the property, they will tell you if you need to add in sprinklers or not. And if so, this alone could add about $40,000 to your overall project.

A very general rule of thumb – meaning don't just assume this applies to you without checking – is sprinklers are going to be needed if your barn is over 5,000 square feet, or has over 300 people, or has more than one story. If any of those conditions apply, you will probably have to install them.

Here's another important thing to mention – Planning Department people are humans too. Too many people have bad experiences working with the planning department because they did something that wasn't allowed and then got their hands slapped.

Planning departments are not out to get you or take away your liberties or kill your dreams. If you go into your meeting prepared, open-minded, and ready to partner with them, trust me – you will have a friendly relationship from day one that will benefit you throughout your business career.

If you avoid the planning department and wait for the Code Enforcement people to drag you into the office or slap you with a fine, you will be stressed out and have a harder time having fun running your wedding business.

Do not skip this step! Having your legal ducks in a row before you launch your business is crucial if you're going to have a future. It's vital for one main reason – if you start a venue business on your land, farm, or property and it is not a legal operation, you will be setting yourself up for some major trouble. And I'm not just talking about possible fines from the County or Municipal government. I'm talking about being forced to cancel wedding bookings and then refunding thousands of dollars in deposits. Not only will this hurt you financially, but you'll find yourself responsible for ruining a major life event for all those families and damaging your reputation.

Plus, local news reporters love doing human impact stories about couples whose dream wedding was ruined by a no-good wedding venue owner who took their money and then shut down. I have seen that in my area several times. You can't come back from that kind of coverage.

Be prepared for the to-do list from the County or City to feel daunting. Also, know that avoiding that discomfort is why some people scrap the idea of doing a wedding venue. This is why I want to tell you that if you can put the pieces together, you will be well on the way to creating a very successful and lucrative business.

To make this effort feel less overwhelming, I recommend you hire a local architect to help you prepare the drawings and supporting documents for review and assist you in submitting them. They also can assist with planning the improvements and completing the construction budgets.

And you don't need to hire a big fancy downtown firm. Many great, work-at-home architects have zero staff, low-overhead, so their fees are incredibly fair and affordable. In my experience, a good, local architect is worth their weight in gold.

Also, remember – since most people quit when they find out the work at this stage, you're already ahead of the game if you persevere. Think about all the local competition that gave up at the first hurdle. And that's a good thing!

How to Evaluate Potential Properties

Shortly after I published my book in 2016, I started to get emails from people curious about choosing properties if they didn't own one already. And to be honest, I hadn't expected that response from people. I set out to write a book for those who already had a property or farm and were thinking about earning extra money. But now, here I was, answering this question for many people.

So, now I get a chance in this book to help people figure out how to choose a property to buy to open a wedding venue business on it. And again, this is not a question with a one-size-fits-all answer. It's mostly because it depends on a few questions you have to ask yourself and the information you have from the jurisdiction you are looking to do business in. But let's go ahead and cover what you should do to help you find the property if you don't already own one.

Step 1 is to find a county or location that allows for rural wedding venues to operate. I realize that is a repeat of some sort, but a legal venue operation is important, right? And so, this step is very much like the first step you take when you already own a property. But if you don't know an area very well, instead of going straight to the local planning department, you can start by researching other wedding venue properties and see where they are. We will talk more about competitor research later, but for now, this is top-level stuff.

Now, I just told you that just because other venues exist doesn't mean they exist legally. On the other hand, you might find out the area you want to live in doesn't have any, what's next? Now contact the planning department that oversees these properties and ask them: what are the rules I need to know about having a wedding venue business on my property? If the answer is that they are allowed, and they give you the basics you need to know about life safety, traffic, sanitation, then you have a green light for the next step.

However, if they say no, but you still want to give it a go because you love the area and think there's potential, then the end of this chapter will be of particular interest for you. Until then, let's keep going.

Step 2 in deciding how to choose a property is based solely on your plans and vision for this business. So, go back to your reason "why" for doing this and the lifestyle you want. If your lifestyle doesn't include spending the next 1-4 years project managing and spending money on renovations or new construction, then it makes sense you should steer clear of properties that will demand that.

Now, that doesn't mean that a property with all the buildings you think you can use for your venue will cut that effort out. That assumption is a mistake that many venue owners make because they assume an existing building can be easily converted to something you can use in the venue. It's not that easy.

I was asked to consult a woman looking at purchasing a farm that the owner had "converted to a venue," complete with a renovated barn, parking lot, and restrooms. The real estate agent had even advertised and priced the property as a turn-key venue business.

However, during my very quick and easy online research of property permitting history, I found the owner never received any permits or certificate of occupancies for the property to be used as a venue, ever, even though he did run a business on the property.

So, it looked like a great deal on paper and to the untrained eye because there was a history of business activity, and the real estate agent was promoting it that way. But what I had to explain to my client was that all of the costs to make sure that the renovations met code (and I was concerned that the barn work did not) and to secure the permits required for it to be a real, legally operating venue would be all on her.

And so, paying this guy for the value he didn't add to the property made zero sense. The property was just another farm without the permits, and the purchase price should have reflected that not the over-priced value he thought he should get. Plus, there wasn't a fire hydrant anywhere near the property or other water source for a sprinkler system. But this owner converted the barn he'd into a three-story wood structure with no sprinklers, no ADA access, and limited exits. Based on my experience with codes, this was a downright frightening prospect to me!

And the work she might have to do to tear out some of his unpermitted "improvements" was a nightmare in the making. She was bummed because it turned out to be too good to be true. But on the other hand, she was grateful that she'd avoided a very costly mistake.

Now that brings us to the next important step in figuring out what properties to choose, and that is your budget for not just purchasing but also renovating them to get to them operating as a venue business.

Because if you decide you want to have permanent structures or they are required for toilets, changing rooms, and other indoor areas, you have to know how much money you will have to pay for the construction or renovation of these places into legally permitted structures for the business.

Once you have your budget and have an idea of what that will get you, it will narrow down your properties. And, again, your county will tell you what you need at a minimum for your venue. Even though people buy this book hoping I will, I can't tell you that.

So, here's another mistake people make when looking at properties with structures: That old buildings don't need to be renovated because they can be "grandfathered" into codes. Nope. Not true. Here's why.

When you take a building constructed for one use or purpose and convert that use to something else, the building must be updated to meet the current codes for that new use. And if the building's new use is for it to be occupied by people, like an assembly space, then the building needs something called the Certificate of Occupancy. This is an inspection by the City or County's Fire Marshall's office, done every year, that the space is safe for people to be in.

For example, a farm has barns built to store agricultural equipment, hay, or livestock, not humans. Therefore, once you decide to put a wedding inside one, you are changing the use from agriculture to an Assembly space, and it doesn't matter how old the barn is. It's getting updated from a barn to a venue. No exceptions. Why? Because it's about the safety of people, plain and simple. And it's about making sure the space is accessible to everyone, including those who need assistive devices like wheelchairs or grab bars.

So, when you are looking at properties that have structures, and you know going in that they will have to be renovated to meet current codes, you start to get particular about how well these buildings are constructed. That is because the better the construction or condition, the less work required to bring them up to code.

Therefore, it pays to know about life safety and ADA requirements for spaces, as I outlined earlier in this chapter. This way, you can walk through spaces with a checklist to see if a space will work or not and how much work may be required.

Now, I covered what you need for a venue in terms of features and services. I want to make sure that you know you can start with less if you have a long-term vision and have to bootstrap your renovations because you might be in a place where you won't be able to get a $50,000-$100,000 loan to pay for new buildings or renovations right away.

And yes, that's about what I would plan for that, including architect's fees and permitting costs. Suppose you can do it for less – awesome. However, plan for double what you think you can do it for if you try to do it all yourself. Construction is always fraught with cost-overruns, unseen conditions, delays, and so on. I have spent over twenty years in construction, and there is always a line item in every construction budget I've reviewed, whether it's a single-family home or a 30-story hotel. It's for contingencies because nothing goes according to plan. Ever.

And for a small business like yourself, the worst thing is to think you can do it for less, get started, and find out it will cost you more and you don't have more. So, you are forced with only two choices: scramble to find more or stop the bleeding by quitting and lose the money you already sank into the venture. That really sucks.

My rule of thumb is to figure everything will cost you double what you think and take you four times as long to finish. I know some of you might think that is pretty extreme, but I will tell you that it is surprisingly accurate for projects like this.

That means, for example, if you have a home equity line of $50,000 to pay for renovations, only plan for projects that are $25,000 total to be safe. Now, if you meet the budget, then congratulations. You have money left over and peace of mind. And you also protected yourself by not using up all of your extra resources on day one, giving you some safety in case you need it for emergencies in the future.

Now, if you don't have any money for the start-up costs of prepping a property for a full-scale venue operation, you can still probably get started by phasing in what you can do and save up for the next phase. There is wisdom in not taking out excessive amounts of debt if you can avoid it.

For example, if you want to start simple and just be an outdoor ceremony site with no changing areas and have a large tent zone for a reception area off to the side, that's a great start. However, you still need a property with electrical power, a clean and safe drinking water source, and possibly a septic system for permanent toilets. If you start here, you have the basics to build and improve on this property if you desire.

Also, how you choose your property is dependent on whether you want to live there. So, are you looking for a place with a home and run a "backyard" style wedding business? Or do you want a farm so that you can eventually, cost permitting, renovate and convert the structures? Those are questions I can't answer for you, but you have to, again, think about the lifestyle you want and then consider how that lifestyle integrates with the work of building and developing the venue business.

In the end, I get asked this question because some people feel like this is one golden answer to this question – that there is a "perfect" property that makes the most business sense. But the truth is that the "perfect" property is the one that aligns with your lifestyle and your financial goals. Once you have that determined, any property can be turned into a venue business as long as it's legally allowed.

Okay, the last comment about this is based on a question I've heard from would-be venue owners: If I can't afford to buy a property or can't qualify for a loan, should I rent it from someone?

My quick answer is No. The reason is that a wedding venue business is location-specific. It's not like a store that you can pick up and move, and the customers will go with you. Suppose you spend time and money developing a successful wedding venue on someone else's property and you have no security or protection, then at the end of your lease. In that case, they may choose not to renew it, take your hard work and do it themselves or find another tenant who will pay them more to run the business.

Or, if they don't like the wedding venue business on their property because they feel like they are exposed to the risks, which they could be, they might terminate your lease because of that. So, if you are not in a place where you can't own your property, it's too risky to take the land/property rental route. Are there exceptions to my answer? Most of them are not rural properties but urban-based businesses located in commercial districts or buildings constructed for assembly usage from day one. The risk is lower to the building owner, but it's the same for you if you cannot develop the business within the time frame of your lease and make it profitable. You can still lose your foothold on the location and be out of your investment.

But there may be another way to secure a property instead of renting. Sometimes, you can arrange with a landowner to carry a real estate contract and set up a purchase agreement. Meaning, instead of getting a traditional commercial loan to buy a property or a mortgage through a lender or bank, you and a landowner do it yourself with the help of an attorney or real estate agent experienced with these types of purchase agreements. That can be a possibility for anyone who may not have the creditworthiness or the 20%

down payment to secure traditional loans.

Keep in mind that a real estate contract is still a legal loan, with interest, penalties, and foreclosure remedies if you can't make the payments. But if you have a relationship with someone willing to sell you their land or property, I recommend exploring this with an attorney.

Now, let's talk about what happens when the county or township says no to wedding facilities on your rural property.

Understanding Land Use & Policy Development

As I mentioned earlier, not only have I been a business and property owner who has started more than one home-based business venture for almost twenty years. But I have been on the other side of the table, working on policy development. In addition, as a citizen and business owner, I have worked successfully on developing new land uses in my local government on occasion, so this is a topic I know pretty well.

Now, when you decide to start a home-based business of any type, you may end up being confronted with two different things that will likely frustrate you and make you hate the local government and the people who work for them.

If you are using structures or buildings for a certain use, you must abide by the building codes, which I've touched on already. These are the standards you must follow that relate to preventing loss of life and property safety and include accessibility, energy codes, and other facets. These are standards that are adopted worldwide and updated regularly by many bodies and organizations. These standards are pretty rigid and inflexible because, again, they are based on safety.

The second thing you run into when developing a wedding venue business on a rural property is zoning and land use. When I mention many times over about a venue being allowed to legally operate, I am referring to the question of whether the zoning and related land use for the property allow a home-based business like a wedding venue to operate there.

Zoning is what most cities and counties use to govern the "uses" on properties, and how structures relate to surrounding areas, open space, and the size of parcels or lots. So, for example, typical zones are Residential, Commercial, or Industrial. In rural areas, zones can be further defined as Rural Residential, Agricultural, or Forestry. These are all designed so that, in simple terms, chemical plants don't get built in the middle of neighborhoods. Or malls get built on prime farmland. Zones are written into codes and laws and used by the government to regulate the land in their territory. This makes them pretty tough to change. Land use, on the other, is where there may be some flexibility.

So, what is a "use?" Well, that is what activities are allowed on properties based on their zone. To decide that, a municipality, like a City or County, generally has carefully crafted guidelines and codes that identify the zones and the allowable land uses in these zones. What is important to know is that allowable uses or activities change over time, usually based on a community's economic or environmental needs. Also, some zones have mixed uses, meaning that some small-scale commercial is allowed in residential areas, like a corner grocery store, for example. Or Recreational uses like parks, swimming pools, etc., can be built in certain zones to ensure that they are located in the best areas for the community to use them.

Why is this important to teach you? Well, because in my area twenty years ago, "Wedding Venues" didn't even occur on the local codes as a "use" for rural residential properties and farms. It was added after the businesses started up, and honestly, neighbors complained because they didn't like the noise and the traffic.

But the landowners made a compelling case for the benefits of allowing weddings on rural properties due to the agritourism dollars they bring to the community and the farm itself. So instead of shutting down the wedding venues, the work started to understand the industry and decide if it should be an allowed use on Rural Residential and Agricultural zone properties. And, if so, what guidelines did these businesses have to follow to protect the neighboring properties and their property values.

Now, changing codes isn't done by just a bunch of people in a planning department office. Public and community input are a huge part of land use policy development. And so, there are often volunteer commissions or boards that work with elected officials and staff members to review, discuss, and create these policies. Members of these citizen-based planning or land use committees are generally appointed after applying or serving. It depends on the area, but sometimes these members serve for a two-year term.

These boards review public input or changes suggested by staff and make recommendations to the elected officials, either the City Council or the County council. The council then typically reviews, debates some more, requests more changes to the language, and ultimately votes to implement the revisions. Once that's done, now there is a new line item in the Land Use code for the planning department to refer to when someone calls and asks, "Can I do weddings on my property."

This is important because often, people get frustrated with the planning department staff as if they love to say no and are just out to get them. But the staff works at the direction of the public. And they have the job of enforcing the publics' wishes regarding how land is used fairly and equitably for as many people and our many interests and priorities as possible.

And so, if you call and find out that "wedding venue" isn't even mentioned in your code, your planner may tell you it's not allowed. But the reality is that it could be if you wanted to change that or wanted to request a special review of your property and your plans and receive a "variance" from the code. A variance is an exception to an ordinance offered on a case-by-case basis.

How people get changes or variances to the land use codes can vary from municipality to municipality but usually starts with an application and fee submitted to the zoning or planning board. You provide your reasons for your request, demonstrate how your business will impact the neighbors or prevent problems, and then see what they say. Depending on the changes you request and your local area's process, you may have to appear in hearings or public meetings. Here you will state your case and educate and persuade people to allow this use on properties for just you or maybe update the codes and make it allowed for everyone!

Again, the rules and regulations are different for this process in every area. So your key takeaway I want to leave you with is if you have been told weddings on rural properties are not allowed or have specific land use regulations for them, ask the planner what the process is for to request a variance or to have the land-use codes updated. They will then be able to explain the municipality's steps for doing this.

This is an undertaking done with a great deal of patience in your back pocket. It's a frustrating and slow process. I have a client on the east coast who is coming up on two years of trying to get a variance on his property, and everything is going great!

However, if you are in this for the long haul and don't care to have your venue business starting up right away, plus you enjoy policy development work, you will find the education you receive in this work extremely valuable. And you will have a chance to learn how local governments work and how important they are to our communities.

7
MARKET RESEARCH

Okay, let's go back a couple of chapters and remember the number one reason given by business owners for why they closed or quit their business: "No Market Need."

So, that's why I will say this plainly: market research is essential to business planning. Because when you discover what your competition is doing, you learn where you have opportunities to offer something better. And while I touched on this in my first book, I decided that during this redo, I was going to expand on it more because it is truly that important, and it is the major ingredient in the secret recipe for the success of my two venues.

True market research is two-fold. First, it involves seeing who is already out in the market doing venue rentals. The second part is, getting information from potential clients to find out their needs and how you can deliver a special experience.

But all the data you gather in market research gets used in a variety of ways throughout your business:
- It helps you figure out what features you do or don't want to have at your venue
- It helps give you the language you want to use in your marketing & sales literature so that you are speaking to the right customer
- It helps give you the information to set your pricing
- It helps you with coming up with new ideas or directions and testing them before you spend a lot of time and money and find out that it won't work

- And it helps you create a unique brand or identity for your venue that will let you stand apart from everyone else – something that was hugely powerful for the venues I had.

This is what market research is not. It is not just copying what someone else is already doing. Let me say that again for the people in the back.

Going out, seeing how other venues look, what they offer, and doing the same thing is not doing real market research. And why does that difference matter when so many people do it?

First, let me remind you that 50% of new businesses don't make it five years. 50%! And most of those, again, says it's because they didn't know what the market wanted. And the other 50% said it was money problems. So, people, do you want to just copy verbatim what another venue business is doing and not ask any questions? I wouldn't because the odds are you are copying a business that's probably going to fail!

Plus, my venues didn't succeed so fast because I just copied what everyone else was doing. It happened because I went out and discovered what everyone else was doing, found out how couples and wedding vendors felt about it all, and then came up with ways to do things differently and better.

In other words, market research is gathering information, analyzing it, and then making some tactical decisions on what your business will do so the business makes you the money you want and gives you the lifestyle you crave. And if your venue business doesn't do either one, you will be a grim statistic too. Guaranteed.

I believe that once you learn how to think analytically about your business and learn how easy and important market research skills are, you will strengthen a great muscle that will allow you to start to see patterns and opportunities everywhere as you go along. And these skills will be very handy if you find new competition in your market and want to stay ahead of them.

So, before you start asking questions, you have to know what questions to even ask. I always like to remind people "why" are we asking the question? It's not about whether they give us the answer we want but rather what we will learn.

For example, with a venue business, it's obvious we already know people get married. And because you already know that people are getting married, what you want to learn are the behaviors that drive why people choose their venues, what their shopping experience is like, and how you can get your venue in front of the right people at the right time.

That's why when we put a survey together to test our venue idea out, we have to make sure we are asking the right questions of the right people and be ready and willing to hear what they have to say, even if it proves our hypothesis wrong and takes a little wind out of our sails.

Here's another difference between the business owner and a person who's treating their business like a hobby. The true businessperson is not emotionally attached to the original idea or business structure. They are attached to the bottom line.

In other words, the only thing I want you to get emotionally attached to is your lifestyle and financial goals you started to pencil out. How you ultimately frame up your venue business should remain flexible so that you can be more strategic about hitting the Levels you want for yourself. So, let's continue, and I will show you how to gather all of this juicy information for you and your venue business.

How to Gather Your Information

To overcome your attachment to your idea – which is normal, forgive yourself – you want to collect information in two objective forms: quantitative and qualitative.

Quantitative data is anything measured with numbers or quantities. In contrast, qualitative data is observed but can't be measured, so it doesn't appear as numbers but as themes in behaviors or answers.

Quantitative research is the easiest to do for any start-up, thanks to the access to the information we have at our fingertips. That means, with some online research, you can kick off your market analysis research from the comfort of your own home office by learning what other people are doing in your area so that you can figure out what works for them and what doesn't.

First, you want to figure out what questions are important to answer to help you start and create your venue business. Some examples are:
- How many other competitors are there out there? What are the standard rates or prices for venues in your area, and what are the features for that price?
- Are there less expensive versions or options to a wedding venue, like

a banquet room rental at the local senior center? Are there higher-end venues out there too? What are the price points?

- How many potential customers do you have available to you? Can you find out how many marriage licenses are issued in your area each year, for example?
- Can you figure out are gross sales numbers for some of your key competitors by seeing how many bookings they get in a year?
- Do you know what the average cost of a wedding is in your area?
- Where are your target couples located? Are they all local, or do they travel from a nearby city?
- What are your key competitors doing that you like? What do you think you could do better?

When you sit down and start to list your competitors, I want to broaden your mind here a bit. Again, you might think that your competitors are only other rural wedding venues like you. But you have to realize that hotels, resorts, community centers, churches, state parks, and every place a person might choose to get married also draw dollars from your potential customers. Hence, you want to include them, even if that's not the business model you are doing.

Open-Ended Interviews

Now that you have spent a lot of time digging around the internet, you want to start to get personal. And one of my favorite and most effective tools is open-ended interviews with key people in the industry you want to work in, particularly in focus groups.

Focus groups do not have to be formal. Focus groups can be loosely structured while giving you a chance to ask several people various questions intended to uncover their motivations regarding wedding venues. Most of the people in your focus groups should be who you assume are your target customers but can also include other people who work in your industry that you might have to do business with, like a wedding planner or a caterer.

You might think about doing two focus groups: one with people representing your potential couples or end-users and one with the vendors in your industry. Tapping into your vendors will help you get an idea of what frustrates them when working with someone who has a similar business to you, as well as they can tell you about the ones they have seen that are killing it. Because if you have couples who love what you offer, but you have a logjam in the middle at the vendor level who hate working at your place, it really won't matter how cool your venue is if the vendors can persuade your couples to go elsewhere. And that does happen.

So, what is an open-ended interview? Well, to understand other people's behaviors and experiences, we want explanations, not yes and no dead-end answers.

This means we stay away from asking our focus group questions like "Do you like having changing rooms available?" and instead ask, "What are some top features you look for in a venue?"

These questions allow the participants to answer in-depth and with their own words. We want your focus group to speak for themselves to have the best opportunities to find gold in their answers.

Here are some other open-ended example questions you could ask couples or vendors:

- Tell me about how you decided which venue you booked?
- What are some of the reasons why you decided to contact the venues you did?
- When do couples typically start looking for wedding venues?
- How did you find the venues you decided to check out?
- Tell me about the type of wedding experience you/your couples are looking for?
- How much did you spend on your wedding venue rental?
- Were there any venues you really liked, but you chose not to book them? Why?
- When it comes to venues and venue hunting, is there something you often wish for in the shopping experience, styles, or anything, but it doesn't exist?
- Tell me about some of the best experiences you had working with venues and why?
- What do wedding venues do that frustrate you but you think could change?

Once you have sat down and developed your own set of open-ended questions, it's important to think about a few things before you jump into doing this.

One, don't forget you bring a bias to the conversation that can impact the natural flow of the answers and the engagement of the participants. For example, if the participants are personally people you know, they might have difficulty giving you the negative feedback you need to hear. Or they will give you great overwhelming feedback to make you feel good, and you might weigh that more heavily than you should. In either case, you will be missing out on getting the information you need.

Two, focus groups are about the individual's answers and the group dynamic. Therefore, you have to make sure everyone has a chance to speak. Plus, you need to recognize when the group is lining up on a topic and listen to what they are saying without letting the whole meeting get off-track. This does require some experience with noting themes and opportunities in the middle of a conversation and knowing how to tease out more data. This is why I have been a moderator for focus groups many times because experience doing this can be helpful.

So, what do you do if you don't have the money to hire someone to help, but you are concerned you may not have the ability to run a focus group on your own?

When I started in the wedding venue business, my experience with weddings was limited to being a bride, so I was eager to learn more about the industry's inner workings. I set up several individual meetings with experienced wedding professionals who were familiar with the region. Each one represented a different experience from working with wedding venues and was also involved in selecting the wedding venue with couples. I didn't want to interview couples because I knew the professionals I picked, mostly wedding planners, had the accumulated knowledge of all of their couples combined. Hence, it was like a 10-for-1 talking to them instead.

Also, as professionals, I expected them to give me the real, objective information I needed to make good business decisions. While couples were our end-user, my business experience told me the vendors in the industry were the source of ongoing repeat and good "word of mouth" referral business.

I came away from these interviews with great insights and saw themes in the answers that clarified what I needed to do to pivot and rebrand the venue. As a result, this backyard wedding business that was making less than $10,000 per summer in gross sales was voted the best venue in the Seattle metro area and earned just under $100,000 per summer in only two years!

If you can't do interviews because people are too busy, you can also send out emails to key people with some of your questions to be answered and see if they will respond. It's not nearly as effective as a conversation, but again, some information is better than no information. For example, you could ask:

- What do couples and vendors struggle with for wedding venue businesses in your market, or what features do they like best?
- What are your top 2 or 3 complaints about wedding venues in our area?
- And what are the top 2 or 3 features/services you've seen at other wedding venues that you like?

I also don't want you to forget that there is a ton of great data on social media and sites like Yelp or Google. Plus, you can go poking around on Facebook groups for couples or vendors in the wedding industry in your area. By reading reviews and comments, I bet you can begin to decode what couples and vendors struggle with for wedding venues. To do this, look for any common opinions, challenges, or frustrations expressed in your market, such as communication, restrictions, etc.

Also, see if you can figure out what pain points, challenges, or desires people are bringing up in comments on blogs, business reviews, or social media regarding venues. For example, do they complain about cleanliness, friendliness, rental hours, responsiveness?

I'd like to say that if you don't want to take the time to gather market research information, that it's fine. But I won't, because it's not, and hopefully, I've made a case for why that is so. Next, we're going to go over how to analyze the information and apply it before we get to use it for developing your venue brand and marketing.

Analyzing Your Data

Congratulations! You have done a bunch of leg work, researching online and meeting some of the key people in your area in the wedding industry so you can make some great business decisions. And why did you take the time to do all of that? Because you have financial goals and a lifestyle, you can't wait to start living, and you want to make sure you design your wedding venue business to achieve them.

Now it's time to sift through all the information you have gathered and perform some content analysis. Content analysis is sitting with the answers, looking for patterns of certain words, themes, or concepts in the responses from your interviews.

Suppose you recorded your interviews with your phone or a camera. In that case, I suggest starting by listening or watching the entire interview from beginning to end and jot down notes as you go, like words you keep hearing repeated by people. Then, take a second pass, break the interviews down question by question, and start putting them into an electronic word document.

Once you have your answers, start looking for patterns or repetition in the responses. An easy way is to use the "Find" function and count how many times certain keywords appear in people's answers. Another way to decode a theme is when you asked your vendors a question about the reasons why a couple finally chose the wedding venue they did. Did you hear several people give similar answers?

You might have to be creative here too because a theme doesn't mean they used the same words. It can be their own words but expressing the same concepts such as reliability or customer service. Once you hear themes in answers from different people, you can start to get an idea of how strong or important that theme is based on how people said the same things.

To do this, it's a good idea to give themes a code and even use a highlighter to mark them in a different color from other themes. This way, you can visually see how often a certain word or concept is mentioned. In this way, you can turn your qualitative data into quantitative as well.

Knowing that you went into interviews with some assumptions about how you wanted to set up and run your wedding venue business, now that you have answers, were any of those confirmed, or did you learn something you weren't expecting? For example, you may have assumed that people choose which venues to tour based on pretty photos on the website. But in reality, it came down to who answered their emails or phone calls first.

Identifying Your Target Couple

Once you have sifted through all the data you have collected from your online research to your open-ended interviews, let's see if you can also figure out who your target couple is. When we talk about branding and building your message, we will dive in further here. For now, however, while you are doing this research analysis, pull your viewpoint up to about 30,000 feet above the ground, look at all your data and ask yourself some of these questions:

- What is the age group of my target customer?
- What is their income level?
- What are my customers' biggest concerns?

- What are their priorities?
- Do they share any common values or tastes?
- Do they have any strong passions or desires?
- Are there any specialized needs you can meet for them?
- Do they want multiple options or services from a venue, or do they prefer simple?
- Do you think you have something unique to offer them?
- How can you stand out the best to them?
- Where are the couples located? Where do you think most of your couples will come from? The next closest city? Your local town? Worldwide?
- What are they spending on the venue rental?
- How do they find information about potential venue locations?
- How many couples do you think you can attract to your location?

You may have more than one target customer. For example, your target customers are your couples and influential wedding vendors. These two groups have different reasons for liking and disliking venues. But you can find that even within couples, there may still be different flavors based on different interests and needs.

For example, a changing room was famously decorated with my ex's dirt bike racing memorabilia of photos, trophies, and helmets at one of my venues. And because of that, many people instantly assumed that only dirt bike people would like the venue. But I knew differently.

So, when I did tours after I showed a potential couple this changing room, all decked out with dirt bike stuff, I would say, "If you can forgive us for liking dirt bikes, we can forgive you for whatever you want to do at your wedding." That statement usually got a laugh, but I said it to set an intention because the motto for that venue was, "That little place out in the country where you can be you." And the unifying theme for our venue wasn't dirt bikes after all.

I saw an opportunity in all my market research that freedom and individuality weres missing with local wedding venues. So, I wanted people to know that we provided a space for anyone who wanted to express their uniqueness freely and without judgment through their wedding. And for some, that looked like having fire dancers. For others, it was to have a deeply religious and spiritual gathering. Two very different couples with a very different marketing approach, but still a shared value that this venue provided.

Don't worry. I will touch on this more in the marketing chapter. Right now, I want you to see how important it is to step outside of your head and into the minds of others so that you can think like your customers better.

S.W.O.T. Analysis

Now that you have collected some information see if you can't identify 2-3 key competitors that closely match what you think you'd like to do. Also, identify 2-3 competitors that are not necessarily the same business model as you but have a big role in your market, like a popular downtown venue or hotel. Then you are going to look at them and do something called a S.W.O.T. Analysis.

S.W.O.T. stands for Strengths, Weakness, Opportunities, and Threats. It is a way of examining your own business and others from various angles to plan or strategize accordingly. It's not quite quantitative because you aren't looking at things that can be measured. Still, it's also not quite qualitative because while you are observing things, you make some assumptions and predictions on your own.

I like using it while looking at my competitors because it's a nice and tidy way of comparing apples to apples for everyone. See, research without organization is just a bunch of information, like tennis balls, all being blasted at you at the same time, making you want to duck and run! But if you have a framework to put it in, you see how wonderful this exercise is and how incredibly valuable it is for a businessperson.

While some people use different methods for organizing their S.W.O.T. analysis, I like to use a spreadsheet organized like this, with the Threats broken out separately:

	Strengths	Weaknesses	Opportunities
Venue A			
Venue B			
Venue C			

Okay, now what? Let's start to understand how to fill in the cells by learning what each column means.

Strengths. A strength is something internal to businesses that they can and do control. So, for example:

- What does the business do well, like a great website, strong online presence, marketing materials, customer service?
- Are there any special features that are better than everyone else's, like views?
- What are the tangible assets that help the business, for example, an A/V system or full catering kitchen?
- What other positive aspects add value or provide a competitive advantage, like a good location or strong social media following?

Weaknesses. A weakness is an internal negative characteristic that can detract from the value of what a venue offers or puts them at a disadvantage. For example:

- What areas need improvement to compete against other businesses like an outdated website, poor or no marketing materials, not returning customer calls, or answering emails?
- What features does the venue lack that others in the same industry have?
- Is the venue in a bad location?

Opportunities. With opportunities, what we are looking for are things you can take advantage of. In other words, think about what your venue can offer that is different, given what you know about these competitors and their weaknesses. These include:

- Is there an opportunity to do business in an area that doesn't have as many venue options?
- What can my venue provide that takes advantage of the other business' weaknesses? If their websites are outdated, can I make mine more user-friendly?
- What do the customers of this venue say they wish better? Can I offer that myself?

Now, the **Threats**. So, I rewrote this book in 2020, and there was no bigger threat to the wedding industry than the coronavirus pandemic. But I have to say I also owned and lost a business during the Recession. My point is that threats are always there, and they are beyond our control.

When you sit down and look at threats, I want you to not just think about your competitors but the industry overall. Then I want you to think about your particular venue and what kinds of things would or could hurt you if they came to pass. Admittedly, this is not an easy exercise to do. Still, we can try to use historical information mixed in with our twisted imagination to develop worst-case scenarios and contingency plans so we can be as protected as possible. So, ask yourself these things:

- Who else could come into the market that could hurt this venue or mine?
- With some of my opportunities, is there a threat that the other venues will copy me? If so, what will I do?
- What could happen beyond my control to put the venue business at risk, like a fire or natural disaster? Do I know what resources I have in case this happens? What are they?
- Are there any trends in the venue market that impact profits, like new competition from new venues? For example, will an economic recession reduce income for couples and lower their venue budgets? Or will venues be able to charge the same or more because there are fewer out there?
- Are there any government regulations that could impact this venue or mine, like limiting the number of guests at an event
- What kind of regulations could change that would force me to upgrade my venue? For example, what if my septic system or well was no longer allowed, and I would be forced to upgrade?
- What would happen if I couldn't do the work anymore?

Again, I'm guessing many of you who are reading this understand why this area deserves our time. An exercise in looking at threats to your business also allows you to become educated on resources you could use to help you address these, in case they happen, such as business insurance policies, unemployment benefits, and emergency funding.

I want to add here before we continue that I realize that this chapter might leave you feeling like, "Whoa. That was a lot." If that's the case for you, I would suggest that you come back to this one again after you've completed a couple of one-on-one interviews, re-read these again, and you will see that some of the things I talked about will start to make sense. I am also sure that some of you will be tempted not to do any of the work related to market research. And if you do choose to skip this, the odds are not in your favor.

Remember the bottom 50%. Businesses in the top 50% do this work because it matters. Hobbyists don't. And do you think running your venue like a hobby will get the financial and personal goals you have? It won't.

However, with that said, don't assume I'm saying you have to do all of this all at once. You have my permission to take a micro-step forward. Make it a goal to call one wedding planner in your area and do one interview. Find yourself time to do online research for one hour and get the details on at least one venue in your area. Even that is better than not doing anything and running into this business blind and just copying what everyone else is doing. Small steps are better than no steps, okay?

8
WEDDING VENUE BRANDING 101

Let me begin with a short story.

Eighteen years ago, I was a young woman that wanted to change the world. I thought it would happen through a recycled-content countertop material I invented in my garage while in grad school. My idea started as a research paper about local economies and then became a passion for starting a purpose-driven company. During those early years, I was able to not only learn the ins and outs of starting from zero to developing a manufacturing company with nationwide distribution and upwards of 20 employees. But I also crafted a unique selling strategy and brand for a product that landed me on HGTV and the DIY Network. At one time, I was also featured in Popular Mechanics magazine.

Sadly, after a series of events that included a Recession, that chapter of my life ended. So now we find me during the summer of 2011, sitting on the deck of my then boyfriend's rural home outside the Seattle area, watching a wedding play out in front of me in his backyard. A couple of years earlier, he partnered with a local florist to host weddings on his property, but two years in, it wasn't going as well as they both hoped. But after watching a couple of weddings that summer, I saw potential. And after the heartache of losing my other business, I thought a new challenge would be a nice change of pace, so I suggested that maybe I should take over the business, and he agreed.

Now, to be honest, I'm not sure anyone would have predicted what would happen, not even myself. I started by taking the business development and marketing approaches I used with my manufacturing company and applying them to the wedding venue business. And as a result, I was able to do the following:

- Increase annual sales from under $10K to a six-figure business in two summers
- Launch an online presence that took the venue from being barely known in 2011 to the Winner of Best in Western Washington's "Wedding Venue" in 2013
- Use the dramatic increase in revenues to help finance and purchase a larger farm and open a second location down the road in 2013
- Immediately be recognized by Seattle Bride Magazine as a Finalist for Best New Venue within a year of opening the second location

But just a year after I originally published my wedding book, that same farm would be the site of a wedding that would include a certain famous computer billionaire and his family in the wedding party and guest list. A name I know you'd recognize. Can you imagine that? I still pinch myself. But the wedding venue experience confirmed that I truly knew something special about branding and business development.

What is a Brand?

We know that the terminology of the word "brand" originates from agriculture and the use of livestock brands to help differentiate one farm's cows, for example, from another. In business, the proper definition of a brand from the American Marketing Association is "a name, term, design, symbol, or any other feature that identifies one seller's good or service as distinct from those of other sellers."

But is this all it is? Nope, not at all. Today, to be effective at winning customers, a company's brand must go beyond a logo and start to communicate meaning about a company and its products or services. In other words, branding is a strategy designed by companies to help customers experience their business by spelling out who they are and what they stand for so that a customer connects with that company and makes a purchase.

In fact, in the wedding industry, an effectively communicated brand can give a couple a decision-making shortcut when they feel indecisive about booking your venue or someone else's.

But how most new business owners do "branding" is they sit down, pick out a name, have a logo done, print the business cards, design the website, and then dust themselves off and say, "There. Branding is all done." But this isn't like branding a cow – it's just not done that quickly. A true brand is so much more than a cool logo or color palette.

Effective branding is applying 50% psychology and 50% statistical analysis. The result of that effort is a brand that becomes a promise to your couples. Your brand tells them, in a myriad of ways – some small and some large – what they will get if they do business with you.

Your brand will not only define the image or personality of your venue location, but it is also an important part of helping guide the property itself in how it will look and appear (now and in the future) to your target market.

For example, at one of the venues I owned, we had many beautiful old barns. We didn't want to lose the natural, worn textures of the spaces, but we didn't want it to be an "old" venue because our target was the Seattle urban couple.

The vision created for the farm was "Country Heart with City Soul." And the aesthetics were a combination of the old, original architecture with modern amenities. This way, an urban couple could come out to the country but not fully give up what attracts them to city life.

For the entire wedding venue business, the overall brand and motto were that we are, "That little place in the country where you can be you." What we stood for was inclusiveness. We were laid back and open-minded. The venue brand was a paradox – we were not like everyone else who has rural farms. We are more like the people you meet in the city, who just happen to be farmers. The wedding barn was a paradox, too – rustic weathered paint on the walls with modern features such as a polished concrete floor.

Now, the key to branding is authenticity. And being authentic also means being vulnerable because it exposes your soft belly. Meaning, brands are made by real people, with real feelings and real beliefs. But most people are too afraid to be themselves out of fear of rejection. It happens in our personal lives and our business.

It was fear that held my ex-partner back from displaying his dirt bike racing paraphernalia and was why his previous partner originally didn't want to have any distinguishing features in the groom's changing room. They both felt that playing it safe was the way to go.

They were both concerned that people would hate dirt bikes because some people do, which would keep people from booking the venue. And if not placed in proper context, it's possible it could have hurt sales. But when I took over, the first thing I did was told my ex to unpack his boxes and redecorate the room right away.

Because what they didn't see or understand was that it was never about the bikes.

When they are placed in the context of a tour, a couple learned that liking dirt bikes is not a requirement for getting married at that location. Remember when I told you this earlier? Dirt bikes were a metaphor for the fact that we all have really important things in our life that make us happy. And I wanted our venue to communicate that we got that.

It didn't take long for couples to quickly understand that the dirt bikes, trophies, and pictures weren't about bragging. They were symbols of the venue's principles of individuality and that we were also pretty chill and not your typical wedding venue owners.

Plus, if the couple did hate dirt bikes and didn't want to book us, that was good because they'd probably complain about a lot of other things too. But, regardless, I knew for a fact that after seeing our unique changing room, people would have a hard time forgetting us. And I was certain people would talk about the venue they visited that had something they'd never seen before at any wedding venue, and the word would get around, which it did.

So, how did I know it would work to use the symbol of a dirt bike as a marketing and sales tool?

Because I did market research and discovered that many couples feel that venues place too many restrictions on them, not allowing them to do even small things to add personal touches to their wedding day. Whether it's as big as limiting their catering choices or as small as not letting their dog be in their ceremony, the message was clear to me that there's a big market for simply being flexible.

One of my favorite memories of the wedding business was when I met a couple who drove a very long way to see us. I can still see the image of the bride marching straight across the lawn towards me with a huge smile and saying, "We've been looking at venues for weeks! And at every place we've been at, we've been made to feel like we weren't good enough, and I thought we'd have to settle. But then I saw a picture of you and saw your tattoos online and said, 'Look! It's a venue with owners that look just like us!' And we came straight here."

Connecting and doing business with a kindred spirit was more important to them than choosing a venue closer to where they lived. That is the power behind a brand.

So, I will cover the basics of branding to help you figure out where you want to begin. However, branding and the science of human behavior can get complex, and you could certainly take this activity further. And so, at the end of the book, I'll share with you other resources for those who are interested.

Finding Your Niche & Market Differentiation

With branding being such a generic term, I want to talk about an important piece of the bigger pie that is very important for a wedding venue business.

Now, branding is extremely important because it helps you identify your company's overall personality and your business. But the second part of my branding and business development strategy is to drill down and start to look at your venue and its services themselves and find ways to make them even more attractive to customers. This is called market differentiation.

Market differentiation is different from what some people know as niche marketing. I mean, it's close, but it's not quite the same. A niche is a focused subset of customers inside a larger market who want or desire specific features or traits from products or services. Businesses decide to pursue or establish certain niches because sometimes underserved customers wait for someone to give them exactly what they want.

Let me illustrate the concept of niche with wedding venues. The larger market is all people who get married and want to find a ceremony location. Then, within that market are a variety of subsets or niches based on the types of venues they want, like hotels, churches, outdoors, farms, etc. And somewhere in there may be an even deeper niche of customers that want to do business with companies that share their beliefs or meet certain criteria. Maybe it's the niche that places a high value on a full-service venue. Or, on the other hand, a niche for couples who prefer DIY weddings. There could even be a niche for couples who believe in environmental responsibility. Or it's a niche based on the price of the venue rental.

To find your niche is like choosing the neighborhood you want to live in and should be organized around the price point you want to be in. Let's say when you plotted out your financial goals; you know that your "neighborhood" must include couples who will spend at least $4,000 for their venue rental.

And then from there, you poke around in that market and see who's there doing what and identify if there's a block for you set up shop; and if there's not, you develop one.

For example, you did your market research in your area, and you find that there are a few venues that charge at least $4,000 per event, but none of them are backyard or outdoor styles like yours. That doesn't mean nobody wants an outdoor venue option. It means the backyard/outdoor venue niche is all yours until someone else decides to move into the neighborhood with you.

Okay, but what if there are other venues in the neighborhood with you? Well, this takes us back to **market differentiation**. Now that you finally found the neighborhood of your niche market, you want to make sure that you can find a way to stand out amongst all of the other competitors who are also in the niche.

Back in 2005, after seeing it recommended by *Harvard Business Review*, I picked up a cool book called *Blue Ocean Strategy: How to Create Uncontested Market Space and Make the Competition Irrelevant*, written by two European business school professors. This book and approach made so much sense to me that I could never see myself doing business and product development any other way. And I've stuck by this process ever since.

First, to know what a blue ocean is, we must know its opposite – the red ocean. Let's imagine the wedding venue industry in your area as a red ocean.

In a red ocean, competition is the name of the game, and to quote Will Ferrell's character Ricky Bobby from the movie *Talladega Nights*, "If you ain't first, you're last." So, the marketing strategy is based on venues trying to outperform their rivals to win the trophy, which is the biggest piece of the market pie.

In fact, in red oceans, the thinking is that there is only one pie of customers and only a certain number of pieces available for everyone, so as the market space gets crowded, everyone assumes that their sales are going to drop. This is why people freak out when they see new venues opening up around them. And the truth is, they might.

Unfortunately, this scarcity mindset and fear of losing and not getting any pieces of the pie make it all feel like life-and-death, leading to cutthroat competition. And so, you differentiate yourself through comparisons and by proving how you are better than the alternative. And then everyone starts to behave like sharks, tearing and biting each other until they wound or kill the competition. All the while, you hope the couple is watching the bloodbath, and they see you as the strongest, most capable option for them.

Hence the term red oceans – a market space tinted by the blood of everyone trying to outperform everyone else by tearing each other down. I would say that it's the blood of only the losers, but the reality is there are no lives unscathed in a red ocean.

Examples we see of red ocean thinking in business are in claims like "We are 50% more efficient than the other guys!" or "Our safety record is like no other." Or "Can you really afford to do business with those guys?"

Now, another common red ocean market differentiation strategy is undercutting prices and making claims like, "Choose me, and you can get the same venue but for 25% less!"

And in that case, in red oceans, your venue price is no longer connected to you and your financial freedom. It becomes a weapon instead.

In other businesses, when price cutting happens, the game shifts to trying to make up for the lower price point by trying to sell a product or service in higher volumes. This, in turn, starts another vicious cycle because if you believe there is only one pie and now you must sell even more to meet your financial goals. Your marketing gets even more aggressive and ruthless because, in a red ocean, you have to steal those sales from someone else. And then the business is stressful and no fun. No thanks.

Now, here's the real problem in the wedding venue business: there are only so many days available to rent your venue out, right? So, you can't price cut and then make it up in volume if there are only a certain number of weekend days available to rent for a summer. And if your price is connected to your financial goals, you also can't afford to drop it, or you won't achieve the Lifestyle Level you want. So, then if you do business with a red ocean mindset, you might feel trapped.

Notice how I have used "thinking" and "mindset" to talk about red oceans? That's on purpose because despite what some business owners think, the so-called rules of red ocean marketing are not really rules. I always think of another movie quote here from *Pirates of the Caribbean*, and that is they are more like guidelines than actual rules. The approach, however, is so well cemented into business owners' minds because they have seen so many other business people do it that they think that it must be the way the game is played, so they keep repeating it. This is another reason I said earlier why you don't want to just copy what other venue businesses are doing.

Let's look at how the real trailblazers do market differentiation – they look for the blue oceans.

Where red oceans are bloody and ruthless, blue oceans, in contrast, are a nice calm place, where you are swimming all alone, untainted by competition. This doesn't mean you are the only wedding venue in the whole county. It means you don't care what everyone else is doing because what they do has no bearing on what you do. You stand out to the couple because you have found an empty section of the ocean, and you are the only whale there, so it's hard to miss you. This mindset is where you realize the market is not a pie with a limited number of pieces. Instead, it's an abundant and creative way of thinking that there is enough for everyone, which is true.

And to get into this mindset, you must be willing to take the red ocean playbook and throw it out the window because, in your crystal-clear blue ocean, the rules of the game are waiting to be set. It is where you get to challenge the status quo and say, "I know that's what everyone else does but do I have to do it that way, or can I offer something no one else is doing and stand-alone?"

Before we dive in (pun intended) into the how-to's of finding your ocean, let me give an example of how it's done. Now, I love searching for blue oceans because it's a creative, strategic process that requires exploring the market to understand what the customers are looking for. But finding or creating a blue ocean isn't always about addressing a customer's needs. Sometimes it is about inventing a way to take care of a need they didn't know they had or even knew was a choice!

For example, when I was in the wedding venue business, I noticed that everyone in our area followed the same rules of offering the same types of banquet tables and chairs with their venue rental, or no tables and chairs at all.

Since I'm the type who is always scanning the market, looking for opportunities, I observed through watching photoshoots, pictures I saw online and in wedding magazines, and talking with the couples as they visited, that farm tables, however, were highly desired. However, farm tables were usually cost-prohibitive to rent and deliver to a venue for our target market. But man, if a couple could have them at their barn or outdoor wedding, I could see it on their faces - it would be a dream come true!

So, I did what I do best and worked up a farm table design that was easy to build, cost-effective, and would look great in pictures. I also noted during weddings that most of the furniture moving and set-up was done by older women like Mom and Aunt Maggie, so I wanted the tables to appear robust and sturdy but lightweight. The tables also needed to seat a certain number of people and fit an optimum headcount underneath our tent. And, since sometimes things get broken during weddings, I wanted a table that I could personally repair quickly and get back into service right away, especially since we hosted weddings every Friday, Saturday, and Sunday.

Then I built a prototype and test marketed it with some photos I posted on Instagram and Facebook. Not surprisingly, the feedback was outstanding from couples and vendors alike! Confirmed by the positive feedback from my test, I built fifty more tables with some help from our staff. But instead of having the farm tables as an upgrade option for the venue, I bundled them into the venue package. They became our base offering, making us the only venue in our niche that had farm tables included with the venue. In other words, the farm tables were our market differentiator.

But it gets even better! Because I also gathered market research intel for this project, I had numbers from competitors and farm table rental companies. This let me figure out a magic price point. I raised the rental price of our venue to a price point just slightly higher than the competition in our area but at half the cost of the venue plus the cost to rent fifty farm tables from somewhere else.

So, in blue ocean thinking, instead of being cutthroat and lowering our prices, I raised them! Now it costs *more* to rent our venue, but couples could get their dreamy wedding image for half the price overall and better convenience, making it a "no brainer" decision for them.

Sales soared, and so did social media presence because quite frankly – farm tables do look great in photos! So, farm tables became one of our major market differentiations and boosted our bottom line tremendously. The initial investment in building the tables was so low that the payback was realized from the profits of only one wedding booking. But the added organic brand awareness was priceless! And how do I know this? Because this was the year we went from virtual nobodies to being voted the "Best Wedding Venue in Western Washington."

I know that a major factor was recognizing that the farm tables weren't just a feature for us but instead that they were a connection to the couples' primal brain. Seeing the high level of emotions around pleasure, desire, and longing for farm tables, I had our venues offer an easy and affordable way to satisfy those feelings. Because we all know weddings are an emotionally driven event and when people want to remember the day, they want every detail to feel like happiness, love, and beauty.

But market differentiation doesn't have to be about services or products; it can also be based on a belief system or values. What that means is if in your niche, if all things are truly equal between you and your competitors, it could be that you are passionate about something outside of your business that sets you apart from everyone else, like, I don't know, dirt bikes maybe.

So, I want you to pull your market research data out and look at it through the lens of branding and market differentiation. Through this review of the existing venues in your location, you will get a good idea of what they offer that you like and want to include in your location. Let's face it: if it's a good idea and couples want it, then you need it too. But, also as important, you will discover what you don't want to do.

Because now, it's time to ask yourself: Beyond just renting out your property for a wedding, what are you really selling? All venues sell the beauty of their locations, and they sell an open date at their location. But the successful ones are not just spraying their brand out like water from a hose to everyone. They are focused on a targeted clientele. What they are selling is a combination of location, value, ambiance, and **experience.**

When shaping your brand for your venue, you have to accept and highlight what makes your property unique. Think about the special needs you will be able to satisfy for your couples. Simply put – how will you make you and your property stand out from the crowd in your area?

Remember, in my examples earlier about my venues. We aren't just selling a date on the calendar. Everyone in the wedding venue industry has the same inventory of dates at their disposal. They all have the basic venue features that I listed for you earlier in this book. But not all the venues are selling the same things. Some are selling killer views. Others are selling their signature catering options.

We also had a beautifully laid out property at our locations, but what we were selling was emotion – the idea and spirit that "Everyone is welcome."

And that is why compared to other venues with similar property characteristics but no real brand, we had so many more bookings than they did. People knew that, regardless of whether they're staunchly religious and conservative or want to have fire dancers doing tequila shots, we provided a haven for them to have the best wedding experience ever. It's the couple that drove a long way so they could feel accepted. A priceless feeling we all want. And your brand can promise that.

9
SOLVING YOUR CUSTOMER'S PAINS

In the last chapter, I talked overall about the importance of branding and thinking about ways to make sure you stand out from the competition in your market. In the examples provided, I wrote about having ways to solve your couple's needs. Now I want to take you through the process of uncovering them instead of stumbling on them accidentally so that you can build yourself a nice, quiet blue ocean.

Before we get started, I want to clarify something for you. While technically, your customer is the couple getting married on your property, I also want you to expand your thinking to include the vendors you work with, such as caterers, wedding planners, photographers, DJs, etc. Meaning, as we dig into this section, I want you to create two groups of customers in your mind: Couples and Vendors, and think about this section from their perspectives.

While market differentiation is an important part of developing a strong brand, I also know finding an uncontested market space or opening one up is, quite honestly, a challenging thing to do. And so, if you are sitting there with a blank page and a frustrated look on your face after the last chapter, don't worry.

A quote I often say to my clients is, "Some experience you can buy and some you have to earn," and in this case, learning your market and the nuances in it as you spend time doing your business will make exercises like this easier to do. Because the information isn't always in what people say, sometimes in what they do. So, you must be watching their behaviors for opportunities, and that alone can take a bit of time. That means, some of these questions

I'm going to walk you through, you might not know the answers today, no matter how good market research you did.

I usually recommend that my new venue owner/operators be open-minded and observant in their first season. This way they can see and experience weddings firsthand on their properties and discover pains and solutions based on the reality of how events play out in real life as they happen.

So back to finding ways to differentiate your products and services and creating a calm blue ocean to have all to yourself. Why are we focused on solving pains? While I'm not going to expand on the science behind the reason here in this book, I write and talk about neuroscience and business. The fact is we are fear-driven creatures with a brain that is wired to keep us alive at all costs. So, it is scanning and looking for danger all the time, even when deciding to do business with a company or not. This means understanding the pains and fears of our target customers is by far the most effective means to understanding how to attract them and get them to buy from us.

When it comes to making decisions about who we will do business with, the pains we have regularly are usually more about discomforts, which are like little tiny red flags for our brain that bigger dangers lie ahead. By nature, we are wired to perk up and pay attention to messages that point out our fears and provide solutions to eliminate them.

When it comes to these pains or fears, researchers have found three main types we all seem to have when deciding on purchases. Knowing these ahead of time is key because you don't want to accidentally trigger these fears or give your couples' reasons to worry about them if you can address them head-on.

First, we may have fears about money and worry about not having enough money for a product or service. We can also be afraid that we won't get what we paid for if we make a purchase.

Second, we also have fears that we may have to sacrifice something if we do business with one company or another. Maybe we worry that the quality of the product will be lower than from somewhere else, which could be a real concern couples have with a new venue.

The third pain or worry we have stemmed from the frustrations of dealing with a venue that won't answer their phone or emails. Or it can be the pain of dealing with a stressful, seemingly complicated buying process. An example of this is a venue not telling you their rental price until you come to do the tour in person. Yea – no thanks, right? And other pains in this area may also stem from a couple's worries of not sharing the same values with a business, like religion or discrimination.

So, if you can sit down and diagnose the pains your target couples and wedding vendors might have and how your business will alleviate those pains for them, you will have a better shot at converting them. Once you have begun to define these pains or needs here, in a later chapter, we will cover how to create marketing messages that will get your couples to pay attention.

The first part of uncovering what pains your couples and wedding vendors begins by looking through your market research to see if you can answer the following three questions.

1. What are my customers most worried about when it comes to money and venue pricing? What can I do to solve that for them?

2. What do my couples and vendors think they will have to sacrifice if they do business with me since I'm a new venue with no history? How can I ease those fears? What do I offer instead that's better than my competitors?

3. What problems are couples and vendors both having with other venues like mine? Do I have a better alternative or solution?

If you don't know the answers, I strongly advise you to circle back and ask those questions directly or dig for the answers. Knowing this is pretty fundamental to branding, marketing, and business development. Because now that we have an idea of our customer's pains, let's use them in the context of creating your blue ocean. To do that, I'm going to take you back again to the market research you did and ask you to look at all of the data and ask yourself four questions:

Question 1, where are venues competing with one another that has nothing to do with the customer's actual pains and needs?

Maybe venues place a high value on the property's look but do a terrible job of customer service. Does that mean a nice-looking venue is not important? No, but it might mean for you that your venue might not need to be as immaculate as you think when you compare yourself to the competitors because what couples desire is a venue owner who answers their phone or emails.

This forces you to ask yourself as you plan your work activities. Should you choose to spend 10 hours a week on landscaping, keeping up with the look of other venues, or spend those same 10 hours on customer service? Which one of these activities matters to my customers?

Another area where new venues get super worked up is how many followers they have on social media. Well, you can have 10,000 followers and zero customers. Or you can 1,500 followers and every weekend booked two years in advance. Social media is relevant and a great tool, but the numbers are not as important as you might think and not worth as much money on ad spend as you might be led to believe.

Question 2, what features of wedding venues in my market are overdesigned and could be reduced because they don't actually enhance the value of the end-product?

In other words, where have venues over-satisfied the couples' pains and couples can't tell the difference?

That last part is important so let me say it again in a different way. Would your customers know or care if you dropped out some feature or service that is common in your market amongst all the competitors? If not, then that is money and/or time-saving opportunity for you to do something else.

I'm going to go back to venue aesthetics again. At our farm venue, it was funny when some people saw that the venue had a bunch of "shabby looking barns." Everyone was so used to seeing renovated, brand-new-looking barns that it became the "standard" for how a farm venue should look. But the people who believed that and followed this mode of thinking missed the boat on realizing that there was also a market of people who loved original, weathered materials.

How did I know this market was there? Again, market research and looking at my target market: the hip, Seattle couple. I saw that they were choosing old warehouses converted into venues and other historic buildings that still had the original surfaces. And until our farm, there wasn't a farm equivalent of that style, look, and attitude in our area, so we opened up the market.

Aside from creating an uncontested market for us, what's the other advantage of the rustic look? Well, it's easy to maintain! Maintenance is pretty much non-existent compared to having to touch up paint on a building that needs to look new each season. Our farm venue set new rules.

The other feature of outdoor venues we stopped doing was "overdoing it" on flower beds. Man. It was a lot of work, and about 50% of the time, little kids would pick the flowers or run through and trample the flower beds! And when we took them out and started to keep the beds as simple bark or lawn – no one noticed or cared. And it saved a lot of money & energy on our end.

Question 3, what features or factors should be raised so that customers don't have to keep making sacrifices?

Asking this another way, why don't people do business with you or others like you at all? Or if they do still choose you, what are they giving up doing that, and can you change that?

I gave an example earlier with my farm tables. The sacrifice some couples made was the pain of not being able to afford them. I solved that pain by eliminating that sacrifice with an incredibly affordable alternative.

With outdoor venues, there is another easy pain or fear to look at. People don't want to get married outside because of the weather. Or bugs. Or they are walking on dirt and grass. Or they want the experience but get fearful that rain could ruin their day and then fall back on an indoor venue instead.

How did this get solved at my venues? Well, the farm venue was the "backup plan" I offered couples. If they still wanted to do business with us because of the shared values but didn't want to worry about rain, I took them to the farm, showed them the barn, and they would book that location instead.

But, since I still wanted sales at the outdoor backyard location, I realized we needed something to address the fear of rain. So, we engineered a giant rain fly that could be set up on the day of the event and would cover the entire ceremony area, just in case. Again, another massive market differentiator that, at this time, I still don't think anyone else has been able to duplicate.

Another reason people don't want to get married outside or at a farm with rustic barns is it's just not the look they wanted. That's okay too. So, focus on what can be solved for people who want to get married outside but won't because of fear. Don't focus on converting people who hate outdoor venues into loving them.

Question 4, what features or factors should be created because they have never been offered before?

These are also a customer's pains from sacrificing or giving up on something that becomes more closely associated with longing rather than losing, like my farm table example again. But because of tradition and what everyone else is doing, no one ever looks to change the way it's done.

Traditional thinking for changing rooms, for example, was that it was just for changing your clothes. But if you think that couples and wedding parties like to hang out and spend the day having fun, you realize changing clothes is a small part. So, one of our changing rooms became a hangout for people to play darts and pool while waiting for the big event later in the day. They look more like a lounge than a dressing room with pool tables, minibars, and dartboards. And as a result, these spaces became an extension of the entire reception area as a private gathering place for people who wanted to escape the bigger party.

Here's something else that wasn't offered by wedding venues in this area before that I'll talk about more in the chapter on websites: publishing your calendar online with pricing so that couples could see it without having to call or email and request it.

I bring this up now because I don't want you to only think about your venue features or services when thinking of how to differentiate yourself. You have opportunities to do that in other ways, like during the marketing and sales process. So, try to think broadly about the couple's entire experience with wedding venues, from choosing one to their big day, and see if you can't find opportunities through the process.

Now, let's flip this a bit and start looking at this from the perspective of the wedding vendors.

I mentioned this earlier, but it's worth repeating here. For a wedding planner, thinking about adding a small private office on-site for them to use during the event might be a real plus that raises your venue's value to them because it's easier to work at your location than other places. Wedding planners often have to change clothes in the restroom and sneak into the kitchen to eat their meals. And they don't always have to be on-call, so they are usually looking for a place to hide out of the way so that they can rest and catch up on work. However, if your venue had someplace that made it easier and more comfortable for them while they spend 12 hours at your location, you'll earn a spot high on their list of venues to recommend to their couples.

Also, caterers have a lot of pain working with venues. Again, if you try to understand the venue business from their perspective and ease some of those pains, they can make more money working at your location. And if that's true, you will be near the top of their list if anyone asks them where they should have their event.

Other vendors who will have good input about their pains and solutions for solving them are photographers and DJs. And no, your couples may not notice how or what you do to address those pains for the vendors, but your vendors definitely will.

That's why during your market research, it pays to interview wedding vendors because they will tell you the pains they regularly have, and what I discovered was that few venue owners ever addressed those pains. But remember, your vendors are a large source of referral business for you, so it doesn't make sense to dismiss their inputs.

In the end, understanding what pains your couples and wedding vendors opens up a lot of great opportunities for your venue business. And that's why I've given the questions to guide you on how to do this as you begin to create your venue business.

The first two questions give you chances to review your business model and how your costs shake out to see places to save you money. Because if you have more money and maybe even more time because you stop doing something that doesn't make sense, you become leaner than your competition.

The second two questions help you see how you can raise the value of your venue in the eyes of your couples and wedding vendors. The questions ask you to think about creating new features by taking care of things that truly matter to your couples, not tradition. If you have things that couples really want that no one else does, you have a blue ocean and increased demand for your venue.

My rain fly is an example of that. That's because the "tradition" in outdoor venues in the PNW regarding the rainy weather is, "Well, that's the risk you have to take." While the answer I wanted for us was, "Sure. But not here at our place." And as a result, I increased bookings during months where rain was a higher risk by solving the nagging fear that kept a couple who wanted to choose us from doing so.

I would also suggest that you take these questions and apply them to some of the competitors in your area that seem to be more successful than others and see if they have applied this kind of thinking to their business and take note. But for now, we are going to bring this all together in the next chapter.

10
THE 5 ESSENTIAL STEPS IN CREATING YOUR VENUE BRAND

Even though we will run through a framework for building a successful brand, I must tell you that brands are organic and tend to shift and evolve with time. Meaning, our business brand can evolve in the same way our personalities do as we gain experiences and maturity. So, when we talk about creating your venue brand, the reality is that not all the parts will be easily defined right away, nor should they be. To start the process of building your brand, I always ask my clients:

Do you know who you are and what you stand for?

Because giving your couples and vendors any idea of how to tell you and your venue truly apart from everyone else will come down to that. Everyone is going to have a nice property. Everyone is going to have a place for a ceremony and some changing areas. Get it? You can't stand on your exquisite landscaping skills and think that it will matter in the end for a couple to decide.

That's why branding is about creating a positive experience and an emotional connection between you and every couple you meet so that they all – whether they book you are not – are going to walk away talking about you. Does that mean we want everyone to like us? No. We'll talk about that in a bit. It just means we want everyone to remember us.

Without going deeply into the background and researching why these parts are important to a brand and creating an emotional connection, I'm just going to lay the steps out and walk you through the groundwork.

I have relied on these five essential ingredients for all the brands I've created in my businesses. And I'm going to walk you through each one and give you examples of how to apply them to your venue business.

One | Defining What You Stand For

We're going to start with nailing down your values and your personal beliefs. They could be about life, but they should be about your reasons "why" you decided you needed to start your wedding venue. Why do you think your venue deserves to exist in the world and be available to people?

If the values your brand represents are not aligned to your target customer's values, no amount of marketing will move them to your brand. Customers build an emotional connection with brands whose values align with their own, which we'll discuss more in the marketing chapter. This alignment separates brands that lead and brands that follow. Think about this in this example.

Suppose your venue is inclusive and you make this a core value for your venue. Do you think any amount of marketing or cool venue features will persuade a couple who is just as strongly against same-sex marriage as you are for them will want to do business with you?

Conversely, how would it make you feel if your customers who kept booking with you had extremely different values than you about environmental issues? And here you are, spending hours and hours, weekend after weekend with people, watching them engage in behaviors that were contradictory to your own?

That's why it's important to remember that if your customers' values are not aligned with you personally, you will burn out and have no reason to feel inspired to want to do the work anymore.

This wholeness that applies to each of between who we are, what we stand for, and the work we do is called integrity. And I talk a lot about this because I believe to be inspired yourself to live and work your business, and imbue it with passion and energy, you have to understand how to live in cohesion with yourself.

Why would you ever set your own company up in a way that forces you to pretend to be someone you're not? Let's circle back to fear and the fear that being ourselves will drive customers away from us. Remember the example I used with my ex-partner and his dirt bikes?

But here's a bigger fear I had, and that was I didn't want to give up my home and property to thousands of people in a year that I would hate spending my weekends with.

So, let's identify the core values you want in your business and life by reflecting and answering these questions:

- What do you stand for, personally and in business: Value, affordability? Taking care of military veterans? Cancer survivors? Are you passionate about environmental issues?
- What are your passions and interests outside of the venue business? Can they be integrated into your business in some way?
- What kind of experiences do you personally want to have while working in this venue business? What can you do to make sure you achieve that?
- Why do you choose the companies you do business with sometimes? What values do they have that you care about? How would you include those in your venue business?

For me, first and foremost, I did not want to set up a venue business that I didn't have fun doing. That is a core value of mine. Having fun. Throwing around high-fives when something great happens. Smiling. And shouldn't weddings be fun?

Okay, so what kills the fun at a wedding venue? Taking away a couple's creativity. Having so many restrictions on a wedding event that you end up seeing the same wedding over and over and over again. That does not sound like fun to me. That sounds boring, to be honest.

Also, nothing kills fun like a huge list of rules and making sure everyone follows them. How do you do that? You chase people around and point out their mistakes. Again, not fun. Not how I wanted to spend my weekends.

The other huge value for me is to be respected and trusted. I'm kind of offended by having some stranger I've never met assume that I am not a capable adult. Therefore they restrict my activities based on the lowest common denominator. And in my research, I found that many venues do that, whether it's forbidding decorations or the big one – hard alcohol.

So, bucking traditions, I allowed hard alcohol at our venues while many venues only allow beer and wine. But, being a responsible venue owner, I couched it with this statement, "You have to be an adult to get married, so I'm going to treat you like one. However, hard alcohol does have some downsides for some people, and there is a greater chance you will lose portions of your damage deposits due to a guest who goes too far. And there will be really sick people at the end of the night, but the responsibility of taking care of that is yours. Not mine. So, if you are prepared for that, cool."

Often, the weddings turned out fine. But the biggest thing I noticed was that the couples all felt respected because I didn't assume right away they were not capable of making good choices for themselves or their family. And they returned that respect to me and the venues by earning that trust I gave them on day one. That is a great feeling that a couple cannot forget, especially when it's so rare with some venues. And it was another way my venues and I gained a positive reputation with couples in the wedding industry.

Two | Creating Your Story

Now, as you can probably tell, I love storytelling. And I know that many of you don't feel the same, so I'm going to give a structure to make this as easy as possible. First of all, I want you to know that this is not an exercise in learning how to write your website's "About Me" section. This isn't even close. Sitting down to create your story becomes a critical part of communicating your brand through social media, your website, and during your tours.

And because it's so important, your story needs to be amazing. Why? Well, because we want emotional connections with couples. And a story without a little drama or humor is dull and does nothing to excite the brain. On the other hand, your story has to be something your customers can feel and experience as they hear you tell or read it on your website.

So, grab your laptop or paper and a pen and use the four questions below to structure your venue brand story.
- Why did you decide to open your venue?
- What are some of the challenges you've experienced so far?
- What have you done to overcome these challenges?
- What do you believe in, and how does your venue represent those beliefs?

No matter how painful you think this is, do not skip this part – write it all out! It doesn't have to come together perfectly. No one is grading you, but do capture it in some form because it will become a script for you in many ways. Once it's down on paper, you can also think about the details or embellishments that add color to the overall picture. In other words, how can you tell this tale in a way that makes it easy for people to experience the ups and downs as they happened and connect to you and your journey?

The story I told when I did tours for the venue was how it all began when my ex-partner fixed up his backyard for his sister's wedding. As I walked up to the ceremony site, I replayed the weeks leading to the big day. As we passed the pond on the right, I talked about how a little idea for a water feature blew up into a full-scale pond with two waterfalls. And once we were standing in the middle of the ceremony site, I talked about the fateful comment from a florist, suggesting that my ex should host weddings as a business. And then here we were.

When the farm venue opened, I crafted a different tale. At the very beginning of the tour, I stood with couples in our famous big, beautiful white barn and told the story of how farm weddings came to be in the Snohomish valley.

It all began with widespread flooding in the 1990s that ruined the historic dairy industry and forced these family farms to pivot. As a result, agritourism was born to help save farms and farmland. And we were here to help make sure the history of the valley wasn't lost and share it with others. So, as we walked the property during the rest of the tour, I showed them the features while I also painted a visual picture of how the farm operated back in the day. And I made a point to talk about how we repurposed or preserved things in a certain way for the wedding venue.

Storytelling is the kind of thing that lets people feel personally connected with you. They get to hear about your hardships and wins, and as a result, they then appreciate and value what you are doing so much more. That's because storytelling is as old as humans themselves. It's how we learn about our history and each other. And once you have organized your story into your journey into weddings, people will be asking to hear it.

Three | Identifying Your Symbols

Just like temples and crosses identify a religion, your venue business will want to have images, objects, and visual elements that help symbolize it as well. In other words, if your brand could only be depicted with pictures, what would they be?

For a venue business brand, three core elements make up the overall visual package. Now two seem pretty obvious, and the third less so, but in my opinion and based on my experience, just as important.

First, what are the symbols that identify your venue? Is there a signature style or look to the venue? Does your venue have unique, identifiable features? Does your venue have a building or space iconic features that are unique and important to your brand? For example, is it the unique view from your property or the shape and style of your barn?

Next, what symbols or visuals identify a target or ideal customer? By this, I mean, are there any editorial or stylized images of who you imagine is renting your venue? How do they look and dress? What activities do they like to do? What do their weddings look like?

I want to make a note about diversity and inclusion here. It is very easy to see our world through our own eyes and biases we have. That means, if you are a straight, white person, as you collect pictures of your ideal or target couple, you may find yourself gathering images of straight, white people. So, I want to remind you that if are building a business where everyone is welcome, make sure EVERYONE is shown in your brand images.

Finally, what are symbols or visuals that identify you and your brand? This is the one part of branding that many people skip, but I promise it is important. And why is that? Well, because we live in a world of deep transparency, and we want to know everything about a company, including who the owner is and what they believe in. We have seen examples where the personal lives or beliefs of a CEO have been enough to either draw customers in or drive them away, depending on the story. So, to have a truly authentic brand that connects personally with your couples, think about how you fit into this as well.

What are your favorite outfits to wear? Have a particular shoe style you live in? What music do you listen to while working? Can these things be integrated into the image of your business and your products? If not, why not? This is about authenticity, remember?

Remember the story earlier that I told you about the couple who saw a venue owner with tattoos like themselves? Creating a sense of belonging is a powerful force in branding and marketing, and we will talk about this again. But before we do, you must sit down and identify your symbols first. After this exercise, pull all these images together and look for any themes that jump out at you.

- Are there colors that repeat themselves?
- Identify the key emotions these images conjure up? Happy? Serene? Energetic? Strength?
- Do you see any objects that repeat themselves that could be incorporated into the branding materials? Crystals in chandeliers? White-washed wood?
- Do these images have a style or composition that you can use as the basis of your social media content or website design?

This step is the first thing you do before thinking about your logo and graphic design of your collateral because this can help inspire you. Further, looking at the symbology of your brand helps you formulate the look and feel of your social media content and website design.

Finally, this exercise helps you define a consistency to the look of your brand across all the platforms you will use and the messages you put out. You don't want your content to jump around from pink and modest to black and bold because the inconsistency leaves our brains to try to sort out the meanings on our own. And if the brain has to think too hard to figure out who you are, it chooses "pass."

Four | Identifying Your Brand's Attitude

Okay, we're on to another oft-overlooked part of the branding, defining the attitude of your venue.

Why does this matter? Because what we say to another person is important but so is how we say it. In fact, we can suffer from terrible miscommunications and misunderstandings when our posture or tone doesn't match the message we are giving. It's like trying to talk about something serious while laughing and cracking jokes. Or being too aggressive and forceful that it causes someone to react defensively or retreat altogether.

So, this is thinking of your venue brand as a person and giving it human-like qualities. And one of those qualities is how it will talk and engage with other people. In other words, your brand's attitude is the general character or tone of your messaging that will create the inner world you want your followers to have and how to feel when they engage with you and your business.

Questions to ask yourself to help with defining the personality of your business are:
- Will the language you use be formal or informal? Will you be funny

or serious? Inspiring or educational? Is adult language allowed or prohibited? And if so, will it sound like a salty sailor or reserve the right words for emphasis only?

- Does your brand have a swagger? Is it cocky and rebellious? Or is it warm and inviting? Or does your brand enjoy being fancy and opulent? Or is it modest and simple?
- What kind of experience do you want customers to have when engaging with your business? Will it be like calling up your best friend? Or will it be formal yet helpful?
- When your customers connect with your website and social media platforms, will they be greeted by friendly faces in a casual setting, or will it ooze of polish and glamour?

Now, let's talk again about consistency. The other thing business owners miss is the importance of continuity between the symbols of your business and the way you present them. For example, if your venue advertises in a way that communicates one tone or attitude, but then when someone visits your website or shows up for the tour, and you come off completely different, that dissonance is difficult for our brains to deal with.

Let me illustrate it this way. Let's suppose you want your venue to be a high-end, sophisticated place of business and all your marketing materials have that attitude. Do you think it would be a good idea to show for tours in your blue jeans and work boots? No, because that is sending a confusing and mixed message. And if your couple was attracted to sophistication, they might be getting a bit fearful that they will have to deal with a dirty venue host walking around on their big day in grimy clothes – the opposite of what they want.

So, as you think about your venue's attitude, go back through the symbols you identified as visual representations of your brand and thought about the voice or language you would use with them that fits them best. And if you see inconsistencies, you have to ask yourself whether or not you're building a truly authentic brand that you can deliver without giving up who you are and what you value.

Now, keep in mind – there is no wrong tone or attitude for your business to take. You can be a cocky and rebellious brand and be quite successful. My venues were a great example of that. You can also be modest and simple and have the same results. The point is that the attitude needs to be authentic and in alignment with yourself. Then, your voice will carry out to the people who connect with it, and they come to join you.

Five | Identifying the Haters

Let's remember that we already took a stab at thinking about who our target market is for your business a couple of chapters ago. But now we're going to figure out who the Haters are. In other words, I want you to make a list of all the people who won't like what you're doing, the way you're doing it, and even people who don't align with your values.

This step has many benefits, but one of the biggest is that it helps you better define what you **stand for** by spending time looking at who you stand **against**. To do this, you're going to answer the following strongly worded questions:

- What kinds of people will hate my venue?
- What kinds of venues would they prefer instead?
- What kinds of people will not understand my brand or messages?
- Who is going to object to or complain about my pricing and why?

Now, once you have these questions answered, not only will you have a clearer picture of who you are and what you stand for, you can now begin to choose your symbology or imagery to reinforce the idea of who your target couple is and who isn't.

One of my favorite examples of this comes from an image I used on the front page of my venue website that shows one of our brides dancing with her friend wearing a full horse head mask. The look on the bride's face is, "No big deal. I'm dancing with a horse. It's cool. Nothing to see here." To me, the shot was perfect for the tagline, "That little place out in the country where you can be you." Plus, it captured our brand in a few ways.

First, the image is funny. And I told you I wanted to have fun doing the wedding venue business, and so I wanted to do business with couples who wanted to have fun too. Second, the image was a great filter. If you did not get the picture, you were not our target couple. It needed no explanations.

So, one day, I'm doing a tour with a bride-to-be and her mom. And at one point, the mom says to me, "I looked at your website. I don't get the picture of the horse."

I shot a glance over to her daughter standing by her side, and she smiles at me, shakes her head, and rolls her eyes. I return the non-verbal message to the daughter with a wink because we both know what the horse means. Daughter – our target couple. Mom – not so much.

This brings me to something else worth mentioning about branding. I have found through the years that some of my older fellow venue owners/operators tend to think too much like themselves and not like their younger couples. So, they have a brand that appeals more to Mom or Dad and not the kid who's getting married. As a result, the venue décor, for example, looks more like Grandma's house and not something a little more neutral. So, authenticity is important, but so is knowing your target market. And the trick is to blend the two.

Another important reason for defining who your Haters are early in the process is that it will help build your confidence. And this is one of my favorite reasons. Because no matter how awesome you and your venue are, there are always going to be people who won't like it and want to argue with you about what you are doing. However, if you have already predicted who those people are, what they will complain about, and you know how you will reply, you will be stronger.

An example of this is a phrase that I used many times while giving tours which was, "Listen, I get it. We're not for everyone. It's okay if we don't have what you want. I wish you luck in finding a better fit for you."

That comment was used when I noticed someone starting to nit-pick the bark in the planting beds, or they looked a little disgusted by the weathered paint on the barn walls and wanted to know when they're going to be repainted. And sometimes I said it when someone wanted to start dickering with me on the price and were trying to get me to give them a huge discount or extra rental hours at no charge.

But instead of feeling rejected or desperate, knowing that we aren't for everyone and we're not trying to be, I was more empowered. This let me stand my ground and not let other people try to convince me to do something good for them but probably not for me and my business.

Now, do you want to know what happened when I said that to someone? Sometimes they agreed with me, we shook hands, and they left to go book someplace else, which is a win in my book because they could have been a pain to deal with throughout the process.

But, sometimes, when someone saw I was the one closing the door on the super-cool clubhouse that our venue represented, a person would stick their foot in the door and beg me not to shut it on them. Because people, by nature, don't like to be excluded or cast out. And from that point, they had to agree to clubhouse rules, which they did.

Now that you have the five essential pieces of a solid brand let's cover the key takeaway from the last several chapters. When you take the chapters about branding and combine them with market research, you will be doing some great work at eliminating one of the biggest reasons businesses close or fail: "no market need."

And how do you do that? You do the market research to understand what the market or your customers need by asking them questions about what they actually care about, not what everyone assumes they care about.

Then you spend time thinking about how to incorporate that into your business and tell them you have it through all the direct and indirect messages from your brand. It's really that easy. But, before we fine-tune this work into your actual marketing and sales process, we will steer the discussion towards money again because your price is also a part of your niche you will do business in and another form of market differentiation.

11
WEDDING VENUE BUSINESS FINANCIALS

As we come back to the topic of money, I hope your perspective has grown a bit so that you can see how important the finances of your venue are to everything. In this chapter, I won't be giving you a full business financial course. Instead, I'm going to zero in on the basics that matter most for learning how to run your own small-scale, home-based business. And I'm going to focus on the areas where I see many first-time business owners make mistakes.

Back in the day, before I took over the wedding venue business my ex started, one of the things I noticed besides a lack of marketing was that the math wasn't adding up in my head.

There I was, watching and listening from my perch on the back porch. I knew how much the venue was being rented out for. Still, I could see all the costs coming out of the business and not enough coming in. And after over 15 years of running companies and supporting entrepreneurs, I was certain there was more money out there.

When I asked how the rental price had been set for the venue, I was told it was based on one of them wanted to make $1,000 per event and the other wanted $500. So, they determined that the selling price for the venue rental services would be $1,500. That was it. So, before I did any work for the venue, I performed a **breakeven analysis**, which is the first step ever in making sure you are setting yourself up for financial success in a business.

I discovered after the operating expenses were subtracted from the $1,500 both partners wanted to earn, there was a shortfall of about $700 per event.

In other words, each wedding was costing them more money to do than they were earning. And it was obvious that they weren't getting enough sales either.

See, the cool thing about a breakeven analysis is that it will help you determine your venue rental's selling price. It also helps you see how many events you have to book in a season to reach your annual revenue goals because those two things are related.

And that's why knowing your breakeven point is a critical first step, so you know what your minimum sales need to be right away instead of being blind to it and struggling to understand why you aren't making any money. And this is also another example of why most businesses close because they don't understand how market need and money work together.

So, we will get into the details of the costs related to starting and operating a wedding venue business. Then we're going to take those numbers, and I'll show you how to figure out how to set the right price for your venue so that you make money doing it.

Wedding Venue Start-Up Costs

Since every venue property is different, there is no magic formula for determining your business start-up costs. How much it will cost to get going is highly dependent on how much you already have on your property and what you need to add. Your start-up costs are also a function of how aggressive you want to develop your business early on.

But planning and knowing how much money it will cost to get your venue business up and running is very important. By doing this, you can create budgets and personal savings goals if you are bootstrapping the business on your own. Or you can use this list in the context of a business plan to take to lenders or investors so that you can raise the money to start.

Now, in whichever way you use your list, I want you to know that start-up costs come in two flavors, and I suggest you break them out separately, as I have done here. First are the one-time costs. Or in other words, these are the expenses you have to spend on day one to start the business, and that's it. Here are some examples:
- Legal and Professional Fees/Licenses like a lawyer to help set up the business
- Building and/or Property Renovations that include construction

costs, permits, and architect fees
- Office Equipment like a new computer, printer, file cabinets, credit card machines
- Event Furnishings and Supplies like a tent, chairs, and garbage cans
- Signage for the property
- Design for a new website
- Accounting software

The other forms of start-up costs are ongoing. These are the expenses you have to spend to get started, and then they become a part of your regular business's operating expenses, which we'll talk about in a bit. For now, here are a few examples:
- Website hosting and domain registration
- Key network group membership fees
- Business Cards and other marketing materials
- Consumable office supplies like paper, printer ink
- Monthly subscriptions for graphic design platforms, email subscription

To determine how much money you really need to start, you must estimate the business costs for the first year. I say that because weddings typically book out one year in advance or more, so you are going to have a lot of operating costs with little to no income for a long time. So, a one-year budget is a worst-case scenario, but it is also a stronger position to know you have a plan for getting through a year with no income.

As you decide your start-up costs, you must make a fair judgment on whether it's a cost for something you need versus something you want. If you want to be lean and savvy, a realistic start-up budget should only include those things that are absolutely necessary to start your business. Remember my tip of planning to use only half of whatever money you have available to start the business, just in case.

For example, in year one, can you start your venue business without building new changing rooms? You might be able to if there are alternatives nearby, like Airbnb rentals or hotels. If you don't have an alternative for couples and market research tells you they are an important factor in deciding which venue to book, then you might need them after all.

Similarly, you might not need to own tables and chairs to get your business going. For the first year, you could tell couples they aren't provided, or you could rent them for the couple on an as-needed basis and include that rental cost in your venue price. That decision could save you the money you'd spend on purchasing your own set as well as reduce your need for storage and labor to move them around.

Believe it or not, starting with less than you want is very common in business. So, don't think for a second that you have to be the perfect venue to get going, no matter what someone else tells you. There is a term for it in business, and that is MVP or **minimum viable product**.

The MVP is the version of your wedding venue that has just enough features to get started and get your first bookings. Deciding what your MVP is for your venue is beneficial from a start-up cost savings perspective. Still, it also lets you get feedback from your early customers on what they think could improve the venue rather than stressing on guessing what you should do. This could also end up saving you even more, time and money by avoiding work early that customers don't value as much as you thought they would. That's why I said earlier in this book to start simple and keep an open mind.

So as your figure out your start-up costs, I want you to think about what your MVP venue is so that you can get your doors open and get the income coming in. Remember, "ran out of cash" was the number two reason for businesses closing and I don't want that to happen to you! And it doesn't need to if you realize that it's okay to be gradual and disciplined with your approach and make sure you don't overspend when you might not need to.

The final exercise in this section is to determine the costs of hiring the people necessary for this business. Remember I gave you a breakdown of the primary roles in a wedding venue business earlier in Chapter 5. Well, to have a person do those tasks also requires money. And maybe you will start out taking on most of those functions in the first year. Great, but don't forget the lecture I also gave you about paying yourself! So, you need to make sure that your salary and the costs for the other people you might need to get your business started. Some of these may include:

- Bookkeeper
- Landscaper
- General Laborer
- Sales & Marketing Assistant

Wedding Venue Operating Costs

Just like your start-up costs come in two versions, so do your operating costs, and those are fixed or variable. And it is important to not only break these out separately but also to keep track of them differently in your financials. I have coached many micro-business owners who lump all their expenses into one bucket. Unfortunately, this makes it difficult to not only understand if you are setting the right price for your service, but it makes it hard to see if you are operating efficiently or not. I'll explain.

First, a fixed operating cost is also referred to as your overhead expenses. In other words, these are things you pay for every month or every year to keep your business going and a roof over your head. What's important to know is that these costs are unrelated to your sales. In other words, it doesn't matter what your income is; you have to pay these bills every month to stay in business. And so, what savvy business owners strive to do is to keep overhead costs as lean as possible. Some examples of overhead costs are:

- Rent or mortgage
- Insurance
- Utilities like phone, power, internet, water, trash, etc.
- Services you contract out like basic landscape and maintenance
- Office supplies
- Bookkeeper/Accountant
- Attorney
- Marketing Costs like networking fees, website, social media advertising
- Salaries for you, an assistant, a maintenance/landscaping position (if it's an employee)

The other operating costs are your variable expenses. These things you spend money on only if there is an event, such as toilet paper in the bathrooms or trash bags. In other words, if there isn't an event going on, the expense doesn't occur, which is why they are variable. These variable expenses are also called **cost of sales** (COS.)

Now, in a seasonal business, some of your fixed overhead expenses like your water and trash will likely increase during the wedding season. To track these increases and make sure they are accounted for in your venue rental fees, I suggest keeping the base cost in your overhead category and putting the seasonal increase in the variable costs category.

While an overhead cost is something you pay for out of the money you have leftover after a sale, a variable cost or COS is a cost your couple pays for. And this is important to know the difference because you get your gross profit when you subtract the COS from your sales price. And this amount of money is called the **contribution**, as in this leftover money contributes towards paying the overhead expenses. You then take the contribution and subtract it from all the overhead costs you have, and then whatever is left is your net profit.

And why is this distinction important? Well, imagine you aren't making money doing this venue business. Now, is it because your rental price for your venue was too low, and your gross profit isn't high enough to help pay for the overhead of your business? Or is your venue priced correctly but your overhead costs are bloated and out of control? Or is everything perfectly fine except for the fact you don't have enough sales? Those are all very different reasons with very different solutions. And if you didn't have your costs properly broken out in the right categories, you wouldn't know which one you needed to address. Now, examples of variable expenses are:

- Event consumables like toilet paper, paper towels, trash bags
- Labor to clean up and prepare the venue for the Event
- A chaperone to supervise the event
- Sales Tax
- Increased landscaping costs (extra service before weekends with events)
- Extra costs in utilities (extra trash pickup, increased water usage, etc.)

Determining Your Price

Alright, now that you have worked up estimates for your costs, we are at the heart of this chapter. I will warn you too that this next section will have many numbers, and if you're not experienced with price-setting exercises like this, it might get confusing. However, at the end of this book, I will tell you how to get a copy of pre-formatted spreadsheets I use to manage cash flow and set prices. Then you can come back to this section with the spreadsheet and play around with the numbers some more.

Until then, let's continue learning about price setting. First, there are two directions you can take when it comes to figuring the price of a product or service and the sales targets to match. You can do it by "Cost-Plus" or "Price-Minus."

Cost-Plus is the traditional method of setting a price by taking all your expenses and mark them up to add profit to it. The **Price-Minus** method, on the other hand, is taking a selling price and working backward so that you can figure out what your costs need to be to make a profit at that price. The selling price you use in the Price-Minus method could be a value that is already established in the market by competitors in the niche you are in, or it's the price you want your venue rented at, based on your financial goals.

For the wedding venue business, often, you are applying both methods to figure out your selling price. And I'll show you examples of both to help you understand this more.

But, before we get crazy, what did I say was the first step? It's figuring out your breakeven point. And to do that, we will make a few early assumptions based on the Lifestyle Levels you have figured out and all the costs you have estimated for running this business. You may choose different numbers for yourself, but I want to give you some fairly realistic examples to help illustrate how you can do this independently.

Let's begin with the Cost-Plus method to figure out your breakeven point. You have taken a look at the wedding season in your area, thought about how busy you want to be on the weekends during the summer, and you decided that your lifestyle goals lean towards only doing weddings on Saturdays, to begin with. So, with a (4) month wedding season, this is 16 events per year.

You assume you will perform many of the job functions the venue will require throughout the year, like sales, business management, simple landscape and maintenance, and even hosting the weddings on the weekends. You know there are a few exceptions for bigger projects or complicated repairs & maintenance on the property, but you are confident you alone can keep your property in decent shape. And with only one day per weekend, you won't feel overworked.

Now, you're trying to keep your bookkeeping simple right now, so when you looked at the overhead expenses for the business, you excluded the mortgage and utilities. Instead, you only added up the new expenses this business would create for you. You figured these to be commercial insurance, office supplies, advertising, extra landscaping and bookkeeping help, and a website. Then when you totaled those, you got an annual cost of operating a wedding venue business on your property of $9,750.

You also budgeted an annual salary of at least $65,000 to cover all household and living expenses, including the mortgage and utilities for the property. Note: Technically, yes, you could break these out and have the venue pay you a rental fee for a portion of the real estate – which you would want to do. But I want to keep this exercise easy to start with and show you how to figure out how to give yourself Level 1 financial peace of mind.

So, your businesses total fixed overhead expenses in a year are:

Total Annual Overhead Expenses = $9,750 + $65,000 salary: $74,750

Now, to host a wedding, you estimated that the variable costs for extra landscaping help plus all the consumables used by the wedding is only $150 per event. Again, you are the host, so there isn't any extra staff – your salary includes your time to do this work. So, how much do you need to charge per event to break even?

Cost Per Wedding to Cover Overhead Only: $74,750/16 events: $4,672
Cost Per Wedding in Variable Expenses: $150
Total Cost Per Wedding to Breakeven: $4,822

Again, not looking at what venues are charging anywhere else, but only what you need to make this a self-sufficient business on its own by hosting only 16 weddings a year on your property; you need to charge at least $4,822 per event. Got it?

Okay, let's ratchet it up a notch to a Level 2 lifestyle. Let's suppose you don't want to chaperone all the weddings, but you'll do the tours and the rest of the work. And maybe on the weekends, you have weddings booked, you are going to go out of town. This means your property is available for weddings Friday, Saturday, and Sunday. Now your sales target goes from 16 weddings to a max of 48 weddings per summer.

But since you are realistic, you want to know what the breakeven is for 30 weddings a summer. And now you will hire extra help with hosting and cleaning at each event. Plus, three weddings in a row is a lot of trash, so you will have to pay to pick up the garbage on Monday after the weekend. This means your variable expenses increase from $150 to $800 per wedding.

Remember, your overhead normally is the same whether you do 16 weddings or 30. Only your variable expenses increase when you increase your sales. However, because you want extra money to get away on the weekends and you are taking on more responsibilities, you decide to give yourself a raise from $65,000 to $80,000

Total Annual Overhead Expenses = $9,750 + $80,000 salary: $89,750
Cost Per Wedding to Cover Overhead Only: $89,750/30 events: $2,992
Cost Per Wedding in Variable Expenses: $800
Total Cost Per Wedding to Breakeven: $3,792

By increasing your sales target from 16 to 30, your breakeven dropped by over $1,000 per event, even with increases in your salary and variable expenses. That's kind of a big deal. Can you see how breaking your costs apart can be pretty important to see what matters when it comes to making money?

Now, let's go one step further and imagine that you are already looking ahead and would like to expand your business someday because you're gunning for Level 3 in the next couple of years. This means you want some extra money available for upgrading the property or hiring more of your work to someone else. So, you're adding a profit margin of 30% onto your breakeven cost to determine what the final selling price should be for each event.

Cost-Plus Selling Price: $3,792 x 1.30: $4,930

Don't pat yourself on the back too soon. You're not done yet. Before we move on, let's review that price and work backward to determine the minimum number of bookings you need to not lose money. In other words, at that rental price, how many weddings will you need to host, without profit, to cover all your expenses?

To do this verification step, now you are applying the Price-Minus strategy for determining the breakeven sales target, and the math looks like this:

Selling Price per Event: $4,930
Cost Per Wedding in Variable Expenses: $800
Contribution Toward Overhead Expenses (Price minus Variable): $4,130
Total Annual Overhead Expenses = $9,750 + $80,000 salary: $89,750
Minimum Weddings Per Year to Breakeven ($89,750/$4,130):   21.7

Okay, I want to review this so that I hope you understand.

What we just did was, first, we used your costs and a sales target you estimated for your business and came up with a price to charge for your venue. And then we took that price and worked backward so that we could see the lowest number of weddings you need in one summer to make sure you at least broke even.

In this example, you set a target of 30 weddings. And you discovered that if you get at least 22 weddings, you'll be able to pay your bills and yourself. You just won't have the extra profit to save for improvements and future employees.

However, if you don't get 22 weddings, you will lose money unless you cut your variable expenses or your overhead. For example, if you look at your calendar and see that since you don't have every weekend booked three days in a row, you may opt to chaperone a few of them yourself. This will save you the cost of hiring the chaperone. You might also decide to reduce your salary to $70,000 instead of $80,000, just until you can get to your sales target.

With this simple exercise, you have given yourself the ability to see your venue business from various angles and give yourself the power to make changes and know exactly where those changes need to be, maybe even before you have money problems. Make sense?

Okay, now that you've gotten this far, let's add a twist. I'm about ready to spin your head a little bit with how you apply your market research to your price setting calculations.

Let's start with the good news. You did all your market research, and you found out that most venues with the same features as yours are charging $6,000 per event. But you just did all the previous calculations, and you see your business is doing pretty good at a selling price of $4,930. So, should you increase your price to $6,000? Or keep it at $4,930? Well, that depends.

You might choose to stay at the lower price because it makes you attractive and your booking schedule stays full at 30 events (or even more) per year. This, in turn, could lower the cost and time you have to spend on sales and recruiting couples. And, further, that could give you more time to do new things or more free personal time.

However, what if you decide to match the market because? Why not get the same as the other venues? How many events would do you need to book each year at the new price?

Selling Price per Event	$6,000
Cost Per Wedding in Variable Expenses:	$800
Contribution Toward Overhead Expenses (Price minus Variable):	$5,200
Total Annual Overhead Expenses = $9,750 + $80,000 salary:	$89,750
Total Events Needed Per Year ($89,750/$5,200)	17.2

So, by raising your rates to match the market, you only need 17-18 weddings per summer to break even and meet your Level 2 lifestyle goals. Okay, but what about the profit you wanted for the future? Well, that is revenue you earn on every wedding above 18 weddings.

For example, if you book 20 weddings:

Total Revenue (20 x $6,000):	$120,000
Minus Total Variable Expenses (20 x $800):	-$16,000
Minus Total Overhead Expenses:	-$89,750
Net Profit:	$14,250

But if you book 25 weddings:

Total Revenue (25 x $6,000):	$150,000
Minus Total Variable Expenses (25 x $800):	-$20,000
Minus Total Overhead Expenses:	-$89,750
Net Profit:	$40,250

And if you hit your target of 30 weddings:

Total Revenue (30 x $6,000):	$180,000
Minus Total Variable Expenses (30 x $800):	-$24,000
Minus Total Overhead Expenses:	-$89,750
Net Profit:	$66,250

Okay, remember, while all of this is exciting, I kept it simple, and we left out a monthly mortgage payment by the venue business, and we kept that as your expense. So, in the end, it's accounted for, but not as a business expense. Move that payment over to the business or have your venue business pay you a monthly rental fee to rent the property from you. That will increase your overhead expenses and reduce the net profits you see here. I will talk about this more at the end of the chapter.

But, despite that, can you not see how small tweaks in thinking about sales targets and setting booking goals plus looking at your costs can swing you very quickly from a venue struggling to make ends meet to taking home a lot of money? I'd be excited about that if you've never done these kinds of financial exercises before.

Alright, now are you ready for the bad news? I'm going to walk you through an example to show something quite common in venues. And I think it's going to illustrate how so many people start hobby side hustles and never quite figure out how to turn them into businesses that provide a living wage.

So, let's say during your market research, you found that most venues in your area are charging $3,000 per day to rent an outdoor venue, so you decide that's the selling price you'll use too.

And let's say you have the same overhead and variable costs as in the earlier examples, based on you doing the bulk of the work yourself. Only, instead of creating a line item for a salary, you do what most venue owners do, and you figure your salary is what you will have leftover at the end of the year.

Selling Price per Event	$3,000
Cost Per Wedding in Variable Expenses:	$150
Contribution Toward Fixed Expenses (Price minus Variable)	$2,550
Total Annual Overhead Expenses = $9,750 + $0 salary:	$9,750
Minimum Weddings Per Year to Breakeven ($9,750/$2,550):	3.8

Awesome. According to this, you only need four weddings per year to "break even." That's easy! So, let's suppose then you take the laid-back mindset of you'll take whatever you get, in terms of the number of bookings. Meaning you aren't working towards a goal with your marketing. You're just sitting back and waiting for the phone to ring. Which is cool because not putting out very much effort still gets you about 12 weddings per summer, so that feels like success, right? Let's see how much you paid yourself to run this business then, shall we?

Total Revenue (12 x $3,000):	$36,000
Minus Total Variable Expenses (12 x $150):	-$1,800
Minus Total Overhead Expenses:	-$9,750
Net Profit:	$24,450

After paying for the insurance, office supplies, and advertising out to the tune of $9,750 per year plus the bills after the events at $150 each or another $1,800 per year, what's leftover you treat as your "profit" to pay yourself, which is $24,450. For a year. Now, don't forget you have to pay your mortgage and utilities with some of that too.

Okay, so what's wrong here? That looks like extra money. Well, there are lots of things wrong here. One, setting your price based solely on what everyone else is charging and hoping for the best is a tactical mistake. Why? Let me go back to the list of reasons businesses fail and submit as evidence that half of businesses close and the biggest reasons are financial problems. And I'm pretty sure this is a repeat: why would you blindly copy another business when the odds are 50-50 that they could be a Bottom 50% Business?

Let me go back to the story of when I got into the wedding venue business, and I had to tell two experienced business people that they were losing $700 per event and leaving another $1,000 per event on the table. Why? Because they didn't run the numbers, and they were underpricing themselves. Yes, I know. Math is hard. But, man, so is running a business without any money!

Okay, what about the venue owners who talk about how this business gives them extra spending money? Sorry, unless they can show me these exercises, I'm not buying it. Based on my experience and the overwhelming business research, people, particularly women sadly, are selling themselves short across all industries. And the biggest way they do this is small business owners, from photographers to jewelry makers to venue owners, tend to count the value of their labor as zero and never include it in their pricing.

And so, what feels like "extra money" counts on them donating their labor to the business. That doesn't feel like a job. That feels more like a sweatshop. Or worse. And I have seen wedding venue owners/operators burn out on this industry badly because the year-round work involved to keep even a modest venue business going never turns into the freedom they hoped for.

As I wrap this big section up, I want to share with you one more cautionary true tale from the wedding venue business industry that I have seen. And that is, taking all the "profits" and using them to keep fixing up your property.

Let's go back to branding, and one of the big questions I asked you was to figure out what venues think they need to do versus whether couples actually care about it. And sometimes that has to do with improving the property and adding stuff to it but never getting the return on the investment.

Think about people who restore cars and the folks who spend $30,000 on a car they can only sell for $10,000. It happens in real estate, too, when people throw good money at bad projects hoping that it makes their property more valuable, ignoring the fact that the market is clear about what home buyers care about and what they don't.

So, over-investing in your property at your expense, honestly, is a terrible idea. Pay yourself. That's a great idea. Or hire people to free you from your work and enjoy your life.

Final Words About Pricing

If your market research is full of good news – meaning that once you figured out all of the financials and see that the market has good numbers for you to get paid to do this, I like to suggest that you set a competitive selling price for your first season. And, by that, I mean try to hit somewhere in the middle of the competition.

My aim was not to be the cheapest place, but I was also careful not to be the most expensive right away. And the reason is if we go back to pains and the perceived sacrifice someone fears by doing business with a new venue. Setting a good first-year price point goes a long way to addressing that fear. As you develop your property into a locale with higher-end services and you prove yourself as a trustworthy venue, you can always nudge your price up.

Finally, schedule regular evaluations of your pricing. I would always adjust the price on January 1 every year after checking our expenses and profit. I would also check out the competition and see how pricing changes across the board for other venues. If prices go up, I move us up with them to avoid leaving any money on the table.

I can't stress this last point enough. In the first five years of running my venues, I doubled the price again since I first doubled them! And what was cool was the venue rental rates rose faster than the operating costs. And, now that you know how to calculate your financials, you can see that those increases are more profit if you stick to your budget and run a cost-efficient operation.

This is an example of another reason why market research is a valuable business owner skill. In this case, it literally pays to be constantly informed about your market!

Having Your Venue Rent from You

In this chapter, I have tap-danced around the topic of having the venue rent space from you because I wanted to keep the financial activities simple at first. But now, let's talk about this. Like I've said a few times in this book, I am not an accountant or a lawyer, and I don't know your situation. So, take what I'm about to tell you and then talk with your accountant to advise how to best structure everything for yourself.

If you do or will own your property personally, then you will want to have the business rent back the areas it's using for the venue from you. In other words, your venue business is a tenant on your land, and the business will pay you rent.

You will want your accountant to help out since some laws exist for home-based businesses to determine the rental rate. But I would first think about how much your monthly mortgage is as well as property taxes. Then I would calculate how much property the venue is using and pro-rate it so that you could see how much of the mortgage and taxes could be allocated to the venue portion of the property. That would be the minimum rental rate the venue should be charged to rent the area from you. Again, run that by the accountant.

You also need to create a lease agreement between you and your venue business, outlining the specific uses and areas for the venue. And then also include who is responsible for the maintenance of those areas. For example, in a traditional commercial lease for an office building or strip mall, the landlord pays community expenses out-of-pocket like maintaining the grounds. These include the utilities that don't have separate meters for the tenants and the property taxes and liability insurance. But the landlord will then actually charge the tenants for those costs with a triple-net expense on top of the monthly rent.

So, you would want to do something similar between you and the venue. For example, what utilities in your name do you want the venue to cover a portion of? Also, what landscaping costs are yours, personally, and which ones will the venue pay for? If your well water pump breaks in the middle of wedding season, will that be a personal expense, or will the venue cover it?

By drawing this clear distinction between you and the venue business, the real costs of operating the venue are accounted for. This, in turn, ensures you have the real numbers to set the right price, and you aren't leaking expenses somewhere you don't know about.

But also, you are creating a clear boundary between you and the activities of the venue. This is another buffer against risks, especially in a worst-case scenario. There is a term called piercing the corporate veil that applies here. It's when the liabilities of a company, like your venue, are then shared with the shareholders or owners, in this case, you.

Suppose you maintain the veil between you and the business by not intermixing expenses and activities. In that case, if something happens on the venue during a wedding, you are ideally protected from any personal liability. However, if you don't have a clear distinction between you and the business, you can be personally held liable and the business. That's why a written lease agreement is important, as well as separate bank accounts and expense tracking.

Now, if you purchase property as a business, which I've done before, this situation could be reversed. Meaning that you would be renting your home and some land from the venue, not the other way around. And that means you should still plan on paying something for living on the property just so that you can maintain a clear and separate arrangement between you and your personal life from the venue.

Again, there may be a few other nuances related to your situation, so I suggest you work up a draft of what your lease would look like and then have that important conversation with your accountant.

12
HOW TO EARN A LITTLE EXTRA ON TOP

For the most part, you should be able to build a quite simple yet very lucrative wedding venue business on your property. However, for some of you, once you pull market research together and take a look at what you think you can bring to the market and how much you can charge, you may have to get extra creative.

This can happen if you are in a market where other venues are underpricing themselves across the board, and the customers are all expecting you to as well. Or, if you have to start with an MVP version of your venue that doesn't have as many features to get you the higher rental rates you need.

That last situation is called having a **low-value proposition**. Or in other words, what you currently offer, whether it's your venue size or features, is attractive to only certain customers at certain price points. We also call that knowing what the market will bear.

This is one of the other benefits of market research: understanding your target customer's expectations and pricing limits. Because typically, if you want to go for a higher-end, higher-paying client or customer, you have to give them what they are expecting.

I mean, I'm sure you'd love to earn a living booking only six weddings a summer at $20,000 per wedding in your backyard right away. The reality is that unless you have an exceptional property - it's not likely to happen for most of you. Don't get me wrong, I don't know you or your property, so it could happen. But probably only after you build your business, earn some amazing experience, gain some killer skills, and develop a reputation for having the best property or having whatever it is that's going to earn you big dollars.

So, after you spent some time looking at your costs, playing with pricing, thinking about your Lifestyle Levels, and then seeing what the market research results are saying, you might be realizing your original idea has to change.

Now when business owners see an idea isn't going to be as profitable as they wanted, before they give up, they get their wicked question caps on and ask themselves things like, "How do I run a venue business and earn the money I want?" Through these types of questions, our business owners end up down the path of improving efficiency, product diversity, and exploring other revenue streams.

Improving Efficiency

Being an efficient business doesn't just mean you do things faster or better; it also means you are spending your money more wisely as well. And one way to see if that's true is through value engineering. **Value Engineering** is the process of looking at your business operations and finding alternative ways to still do the same thing but at a lower cost. Routinely used in construction and manufacturing to look for less expensive ways to build a building or product, the concept can also apply to service industries like running a wedding venue. With the goal of not sacrificing the functionality services you provide, you use this to help lower your expenses by simply going line by line through your costs and brainstorming on less expensive options.

For example, you could find that it's less expensive to have a bookkeeper come in once a month to help with paying bills and other banking assistance than it is for you to have a full-time business manager or assistant. Other cost-savings can be in bulk ordering supplies from a large wholesaler. Or, like I mentioned while talking about market differentiation, see if you are doing higher levels of work somewhere that the customer doesn't even notice or care about that you can stop. For example, maybe you can save money on landscaping areas that aren't used as often as other areas?

As a small business owner with limited resources, you want to also look at the entire process of running your business and see if there are steps or activities you do that can be automated or streamlined to reduce labor costs.

Streamlining is looking at ways to be more efficient and effective by employing faster or simpler working methods. Streamlining has multiple benefits, including freeing up more time to allow you to do work in areas of your business that create more value, like marketing. But it also can lower your labor expenses if you're paying someone else to do that work. In a service-oriented business like a wedding venue, streamlining looks like setting up automated email replies, using social media graphics templates, or standardizing any repetitive processes or tasks your business requires.

Venue Service Diversity

One way to move the needle on how much you need to sell or produce is to look at the different services you can offer and evaluate them to see which ones better meet your financial goals.

For example, you wouldn't want to spend a ton of energy renting your property out hourly if it's more profitable to book fewer, high-dollar wedding packages instead. Keeping your efforts focused on the right services helps ensure you don't spend too much time on options that are not big moneymakers and not enough time on those.

Now, I didn't just say that variety is bad. In fact, having a variety in your offerings that includes lower-priced rental options is a good thing because it helps to draw customers into your business and up towards your high-end booking options. Having different pricing levels in your goods and services is called having a product ladder. So, this means that if you have a few inexpensive booking options and give customers a sample of what you can do, that's okay. You just don't want to build your business around them when what you really want them to eventually purchase is your full-day weekend, high-profit option.

If done right, product diversity can help you grow your wedding business. That's because other large gatherings like memorials or celebrations of life are a major source of bookings for many venues. And as you would expect, funerals are as common as weddings, with an ongoing demand because that's just how life is. The other important feature of these events is that, unlike a wedding you are booking a year or more in advance, most memorials are relatively last-minute affairs, for obvious reasons.

So, you could include in your venue product ladder a last-minute full-day package aimed at elopements, memorials, birthday parties, company picnics, and more. This could be a 50% discount off your standard pricing and be an effective way to fill holes in your calendar, especially in the first few years as you grow your reputation. I would offer that price only to events that will take place in 90 days or less from the day of booking.

Now how does this grow your higher profit wedding rentals? Well, imagine a guest at a memorial steps onto your property who didn't know you existed before that day. Fast forward a few months, and now when they need a venue for a summer party or their daughter's wedding, they call you up. That really does happen.

Another form of a product ladder for wedding venues is to offer different full-day rates based on the day and the number of rental hours. It can look like the following.

Weekday Hourly Rental Fee: Monday thru Thursday, 10a – 8 pm, $100/hour
Friday/Saturday Full Day Rental: $4,000 for 12 hours
Sunday Full Day Rental: $3,500 for 10 hours

There are other details and conditions you want to spell out, especially on the hourly option. For example, will there be limited venue use, like excluding the changing rooms from the rental? Or will you have a sliding scale per hour rate based on hours booked? Plus, you want to make sure you leave time in your calendar for your wedding rehearsals and Open houses and things like that. You can also mix and match a few of the suggestions I've given you here or use your market research to come up with more. But hopefully, from the examples I gave you, you get the idea of how product diversity works.

Venue Up-Sells

I have always recommended that the best way to make good profits from this business is to keep your operation simple and streamlined. However, suppose you are considering making this a business that can give you a Level 4 lifestyle. In that case, it might be necessary to add other sources of revenue besides straight venue rentals.

However, I still preface this with some caution and don't recommend you run out and add these on in year one, especially if this is the first business you've ever owned and operated. And I want to add this reminder that every extra service you provide or responsibility you take on has a reciprocal increase in expenses for you and your business.

For example, renting décor items means more storage space is needed and replacement costs due to breakage. Offering clean-up or decorating services might mean hiring more people to work for you and more time to manage them. However, when you decide it's time to level up, here are some extra services compatible with a venue business.

Furniture and Décor Rentals. I like this one very much because, first of all, I like antique shopping and love crafty projects like re-painting furniture. If you do, too, then this is a very cool up-sell option for you, and it could spin off into a whole other business venture. This is not like a party rental company that rents event items such as table linens, folding chairs, drinking glasses, and cocktail tables. This up-sell option is a niche rental business that offers couples the chance to rent specialty decorative items such as vintage tables, dressers, or sofas. A décor company might also have an extensive collection of unique glassware or vases for table settings.

If you have space to store the items and have an eye for good pieces, I'd say go for it. But start this venture in the same way as the venue business – get some market research under your belt. Specifically, find out what kinds of items couples are looking to rent before investing in a lot of inventory that sits around in your garage.

Now, you could also offer more traditional items for couples to rent at your venues like linens, dishes, glassware, and flatware. I knew a few venues that do, and it's a huge convenience for the DIY couple or smaller weddings that want to have a few vendors to coordinate as possible. They are not required to be used, but they are there to rent if the couple wants them. However, the consideration here is that you now have to clean everything yourself, and there is time and money involved in that. So, carefully calculate the costs and the benefits.

Coordination on the Day of the Event. Unlike wedding planning, day-of-coordination is simply taking on the role of Event Manager for the day of the event only. What that means is the Day Of Coordinator (DOC) makes sure the vendors all show up on time, they get the wedding party ready on time, they manage the timeline throughout the day, handle the parents and the guests when they have questions, and a million other things that can come up. It's a very busy and exhausting job, but some families will gladly pay a couple of extra hundred bucks for you to do it, especially since you will be there anyway. I don't recommend you attempt this unless you have great people skills, juggle many things at once, and are naturally grace under fire.

Some venue owners accidentally end up doing this work because they don't understand the boundary between being a representative of the venue versus the family's go-to for everything. Helpfulness is an amazing feature of a good venue host; however, it is not your job to run the wedding for them, so steer clear of getting roped into it. If you want to do it, make it an option to hire you and be very clear about what you will and won't do. And let me repeat myself: this is not an up-sell. I recommend if you don't have good project management experience, period.

Floral. If you are on a farm or have an extensive property to grow flowers, shrubs, and herbs and love doing it, then you could provide a Farm-to-Wedding floral option for your couples. Also, if you have gathered a nice collection of vases or mason jars, you could charge extra for making the complete arrangements. To grow a variety of flowers requires a lot of time and acreage, plus flower growing at a scale that allows you to service a dozen weddings a summer takes a lot of work. However, if you decide to provide a niche floral service, say by focusing on only a couple of options, like roses or lavender, you might have a nice balance of work and sales and get paid for your hobby.

One of my farms had several acres of flowers grown by farmers who rented the land from us. I connected many weddings directly with my growers for their wedding floral needs and stayed out of the middle. Thanks to that experience, I know the demand exists. However, because of the seasonality of flower growing and the scale, this niche business serves a modest decorating theme much better than an over-the-top posh styled event.

Extra Rental Time. This is a super easy up-sell if you don't mind working extra hours. Some couples simply want to find an extra hour or two in their venue rental period or at their Rehearsal time and will pay to get it. I'd grant an extra hour here or there in the early days because I wanted the extra revenue. But once bookings picked up, every hour of non-wedding work was precious to me, so I stopped.

Plus, my venues already offered 14 hours of rental time, almost double the time of other locations. I could have easily changed our rental period to 8 or 10 hours and then charged a premium hourly rate for anyone who wanted to still have a 14-hour window and possibly make more per event. But, based on the market research, I believed we'd lose more sales than we'd gain in revenue. Our long hours were very attractive to couples. However, if you find from your market research that most venues offer only 8-hour rentals, then you can decide if you'll do the same but offer the up-sell or choose to offer more time in your base agreement and just charge more for the entire rental.

Cleaning and/or Decorating Services. If you wanted to offer this up-sell, I suggest you have a partner in this one. Otherwise, you'll be working too hard! For this up-sell, you can offer your couples the service of arranging the tables, chairs, table settings, and decorations per their plans. You can also then offer a clean-up service for the end of the night that can involve packing up the decorations for them. As I said, this is a plausible up-sell for a venue, but it does add a lot of work to your day, so I would see if there are any event service companies already in your market. Then, find out if you can work out a deal with them for pricing that allows you to hire them, mark up their rate and then charge your couples for the service.

At my venues, we didn't do the set-up or the clean-up, so the couples were responsible for it. If they wanted a clean-up service option, I referred them to a company I liked and stayed out of it. However, if you desire to make another $50-100 profit per event, this is probably an easy up-sell because of the convenience and the fact that everyone hates cleaning! But I'd run those numbers and make it worth it for you. It's exhausting at the end of the day, and I couldn't wait to shut the lights off and go to bed, so I was personally grateful that the couples or professionals came in to pack the mess up and left.

Catering. Okay, this is a big upsell and pretty complex, but there are many venues out there that caterers own. So, if you were ambitious and have access to a full-scale commercial kitchen, you could offer catering with your venue. If any up-sells truly elevate venues from mid-level to the high end, it is having catering included. There are many ways to do this, from being the caterer yourself or partnering with a company. This is different from having a preferred list of caterers you work with. What I'm talking about here is including the cost of food into the venue rental so that it's an all-in-one package. Again, a complicated up-sell unless you happen to be a restaurateur or caterer already.

Vendor Packages. In a similar vein, some venues offer package deals with other vendors, like planning and photography, so you might explore that. However, I would use market research to guide this decision. Most couples I found prefer flexibility in choosing vendors. But for some who want simplicity, this might not be a bad option, but an up-sell is only an up-sell if it actually increases your bottom line. This is why when I was approached by vendors who wanted me to offer my couples vendor packages if the vendors didn't give me a financial reason to say yes, I didn't. That means your bundle should be something that offers a couple a convenience they are willing to pay a little extra for. So, what would you offer that does that and gives you some extra money for the effort? Otherwise, there's no point.

Live Streaming. Finally, a possible up-sell for venues in a post-coronavirus world that I've mentioned already briefly would be to offer live streaming capabilities for any event. This involves installing web cameras in key locations and having them all wired back to a central location for someone to bring in their laptop to connect. To do this effectively, you also need to make sure that you have the extra bandwidth from your internet provider so that there aren't any delays or loss of connection. You could allow a couple to use the equipment if they have their tech person and not charge for the use. That's a pretty cool feature that is not apt to go away if you ask me. However, if they are not tech-savvy but love the idea of having virtual wedding guests, you will need to have a person on hand to set it up, manage it and make sure it works, and that should be something you charge for.

So, there you go—a few ideas on how to add some extra money on top of your standard rental services. Now, aside from the improvements to your efficiency, I want to again encourage first-time venue or business owners to keep things simple in the first year or two. But, once you gain confidence, experience in your market and with your couples, I bet there are some extras you can and should consider that will help you build a truly profitable venue business.

13
MARKETING & SALES BASICS

Alright, now we are getting into one of my favorite topics: marketing. In fact, when I look at the word count for the original book, this section represented almost one-third of the entire book. Aside from the financials, that's how important this topic is to the success of your venue business. Because this is where we take all the great work you did on market research and forming your brand and then blast it out there and start bringing couples in. So, to do that, let's first learn about something called the **Buyer's Journey**. The Buyer's Journey is the process of realizing we need something, whether it's new running shoes or a wedding venue, to the point of actually making that choice and spending the money.

When we knew we needed something like clothes or a new car but didn't know what we wanted, we hit the streets back in the day. We might wander around shops and malls, from store to store, window shopping until we saw something we liked and then went into the store to buy it. Or we'd go someplace like a car lot and let the salesperson educate us on the features of the vehicle we might be considering.

In the wedding industry old days, couples on their journey would use wedding magazines to get all their information about planning a wedding. Then once they had an idea of what they wanted, a couple might hit the Yellow pages in the phone book (anyone remember that?) or head over to the local wedding show to find out who in the area could provide the services they needed. Also, it's worth noting that most people got married at traditional venues like their church, temple, or synagogue. So, venue hunting wasn't even really a thing back then. However, as we know, big shifts have happened in the last twenty years across the board in this field. And one of the biggest is how we shop.

Today, we don't have to leave our homes to learn everything we want to know about a product, service, or company. Research shows that most of us will do online research before we take the next steps to go to a store or make a purchase. So, what has been critical in the past two decades has been for businesses to move away from the old buying habits of consumers and shift to meet their customers online, even if they are physical brick-and-mortar businesses.

Now, I want to be clear here, while the methods of finding our information have changed, the Buyer's Journey hasn't. And that's because the Journey is based on the psychological experience we have as we make decisions. So, that's the key thing to remember here. The Buyer's Journey comprises three key stages, and at each stage, it is important to understand the couple's mindset and tailor your marketing to give them what they want at that time. So, let's review them.

Stage 1 Awareness. This is the point at which a couple has gotten engaged, and now they are asking themselves, "Where are we going to get married?" And that's when they hit the internet and begin searching. They are looking for all the wedding venue options and seeing how other people are getting married. Through this process, they start to get a feel for all the different places a couple can get married at, and during this stage, you want to make sure your venue shows up in their search results.

Stage 2 Consideration. After all the initial work, the couple has identified their shortlist of options based on what they believe are the most important features they want from a wedding venue. So, at this stage, they are now comparing venues with these options & features against each other to see who they want to visit and learn more about. Because it's the comparison stage, they need the information to do that, so you have to be able to provide it.

Stage 3 Decision. Now – it gets good! This is where the couples are reaching out and ready to meet you and see the venue in person. They want their venue booked and their date secured. And they want to do business with a place that will help them realize their dream wedding. Now, they might still be considering and comparing you to some other places. But, if you've put good information out there on the internet for them to find, there is a good chance they learned everything they needed to know about your venue, what you stand for, what a wedding with you will be like, and have already made up their mind. So now they just want to come to the property to verify their choice and sign the contract. That happened a lot with my venues.

With these three stages, I want you to remember that your marketing messages and content are different during the Journey. That means there is a deliberate pace you have to walk couples through that ensures you can escort the couple through their decision-making process. And if you do this successfully, you will walk them right up to your front door, and they will book you.

Creating Awareness with Couples

Let's touch again on the fact that wedding venues have two buckets of customers – couples and other wedding vendors. Couples are the ones who use your services one time, but that doesn't mean they have limited influence. They can be a source of referrals for their friends and family. Also, the guests at their wedding are potential future couples – I've seen that many times. And the wedding guests become direct or indirect referrals every time they post pictures on social media of their best friend's wedding at that awesome venue outside of town.

Vendors, on the other hand, are repeat business, quite literally. Depending on your area, you may end up seeing the same DJs, wedding planners, caterers, and photographers at your venue regularly. Sometimes the reason is that these people were all a part of a wedding once that got published. Then other couples, dying to capture that same magic for theirs, hire the same team. Or the vendors like working with you and your location, so they make sure to mention you to the couple that hasn't picked a location yet.

Now again, the Awareness stage on the Buyer's Journey for a couple or a vendor is the point at which they recognize they have a need. In the case of the couple who just got engaged, now they need to figure out where to have their wedding. But your problem is that they may not know you even exist. So how does a couple learn about you during this stage? Well, it usually happens one of four ways:

1. They find you online while doing generic searches about weddings, venues, and other things.
2. A vendor refers you to them
3. A past customer or guest tells them about you
4. They see you at a local wedding show

Now, since you don't have guests or customers yet, the top two ways to get your name out in the industry are #1 and #2. But before I move on, I will touch on #4. Wedding shows have some value, but it depends on the show, the location, and the structure. To participate in a wedding show is costly and, in my experience, the return on investment was really low. You have to have an eye-catching booth designed to do a wedding show, which takes time and money. Plus, the day you spend setting it up, the days you spend standing at it during the show, and the day you spend packing up and going home. Not to mention you also probably paid a few hundred dollars just to be at the show.

If there were tons of visitors looking for venues, it's not a bad deal if you can come out of it with a couple of bookings. However, wedding shows at the local convention center have been in decline for a few years. And now, after social distancing due to the pandemic, the future for them is uncertain, which is why I'm saying to just not bother with them at the moment. Because do you want to know what's not in decline? The internet.

So, let's talk about online searches and how to build awareness for your venue there because, as you recall, we all - not just couples - hit the internet and do a ton of research before making any big purchase. And how the mysteries of the internet search process works are through keywords and search terms. You type, and then the search engine gods find all the places on the internet where the keywords you typed in show up. It's that easy.

But if you are a venue and the couple doesn't know who you are yet, how do you show up in search results? First, put yourself in the couple's seat and imagine what you would type into a browser search bar if you were learning about wedding venue options during the Awareness stage. These search terms might look like these:

- Wedding venues near me
- How to choose a wedding venue?
- How much do wedding venues charge?
- What venues allow dogs?

Aside from using your imagination, you can use your market research to help you figure out what these key search terms or phrases are. In fact, at my tours, I would ask couples how they found us, and I'd take note of where they got the information and what search phrase they used.

Why do we care about these search terms and phrases? The first reason is that when you type in these phrases, you want to see what shows up on that first page of results. And then you want to get yourself wiggled into those websites if you can. Those search phrases also get worked into your copy so that the search engines can match what the couple typed in with your venue. The more closely your written content matches the search phrases used by couples, the higher the chances are you will show up on page one results. This is what is meant by SEO or Search Engine Optimization.

Now, content is not just the copy or words on your website, but it's also the written descriptions you use everywhere about your venue, articles you publish, social media posts, and so on. Creating awareness is like casting a giant net out there and getting as many couples to see you and your venue as possible. Only, in this case, you are not the fisherman – you are the fish! And to increase your chances of being caught in their worldwide research, you have to do the work to be seen more than one time in more than one place, so much so that they want to check out your website. Being everywhere online is a form of psychological verification that helps you look more legitimate than a venue that doesn't.

Being seen everywhere then starts with looking at those page one results and seeing who showed up. And I would bet, for the most part, they are wedding planning websites like WeddingWire, The Knot, or the Venue Report. And so, step zero in creating awareness is to go get your venue listed on all the wedding planning websites. All of them.

Some of them have free listing options and, for your new business, those will work just fine. In fact, because you are new and won't have many weddings to showcase yet, it's not a good use of your money to pay for advertising when you don't have much to show anyone.

But don't get lazy with your descriptions and photos. Think about your brand and your story and put some effort into a selling description of your venue. Don't worry if it's not perfect on day one; you can always go back and polish it. But remember that in the awareness stage, you are being compared to others, so include the features that make you special that will catch your couples' eye so that they don't pluck you out of the net and throw you back into the ocean.

Using Social Media to Create Awareness

First, I'm not going to go into the "How To" of each social media platform I'm going to talk about because the algorithms and designs change so frequently that this book wouldn't age well. So, the key takeaway from this section is to be proficient with these platforms and have a plan for staying up to speed on changes.

Instead, I will simply share the ones that have been most successful for the venues I've owned. Now social media channels come in two varieties – ones where you go for inspiration and conversations. And in the wedding world, there are three big players here: Instagram, Facebook, and Pinterest.

First, **Instagram.** This platform is for inspiration and what I call mild conversation. And in the early days of your venue, you won't have a ton of inspiring wedding pictures to share. But that's okay because you can inspire in other ways. If you go back to branding and recall the importance of storytelling, Instagram is a place for you to tell the story of your venue and its beginnings through photos.

These can be photos of the venue under its transformation and pictures of you working on it, for example. You can also share photos that have inspired you that illustrate your dreams and plans for the venue. If you have a historic property, these can be fun for people to follow along with and watch the metamorphosis. One of my clients is a historic mansion in Bucks County, Pennsylvania, that hasn't hosted a wedding yet, but they already have over 4,000 followers on their Instagram.

For weddings and Instagram, it's important to remember that people come to Instagram to see beautiful pictures. That means even if you're plugging your venue journey, I would still use high-quality images for your feed and go casual in your Stories. Oh, and don't forget to tag your photographers!

Now **Facebook** is a social media platform for conversations. And as such, using Facebook is not just setting up your venue business Page and posting about your business. To get the most out of Facebook to create awareness for your venue means you have to butt into the discussions. You do this by joining the wedding planning Facebook groups that exist in your area – and they are there! These groups are where couples crowdsource from each other and wedding vendors for information and tips. So, in the Facebook search bar, type in "Weddings" and add in your city or county, then sort the results. You can see what people are posting, what Groups are out there to join, and who else is in your area in the wedding industry.

Finally, **Pinterest** is the goddess of inspiration platforms for the wedding industry but might be the most underutilized or misused by venues. When I attended a wedding conference a couple of years ago, one of the seminars I went to give the low-down on social media research. The presenter, the head marketing guy from one of the biggest online wedding websites, found that before couples go-to wedding planning sites like theirs, they start on Pinterest. That's how big this platform is for you.

The mistake I see businesses make is that they pin other people's stuff but forget to upload their original content with a backlink to their website. One wedding organization I consulted for had thousands of pins and boards on their Pinterest account. Unfortunately, as I reviewed them, I found that barely any of were original content highlighted the vendor members of the organization. So, while someone had fun searching and pinning, the account didn't have the impact on the members it could have had.

On the other hand, Pinterest works when you upload your photo, with the proper photo credit to the photographer. Then you add keywords and descriptions to make it easy to find during a search, and you include your website. Then, when someone sees the picture and they re-pin it, now your name is traveling with the picture every time it's re-pinned.

So, if you simply share someone else's pin, once the picture is re-pinned again, you are cut out of the thread. That's because the credit stays with the original post. And that is why you have to have your pictures or graphics on Pinterest.

New social media platforms have come and gone since I originally published my book, and all business owners struggle with keeping up or deciding if they need to learn a new trick. For example, in 2014, it was insisted by a wedding consultant once that Snapchat was a must for venues because the target user was the same age as the couples. Before that – Vine. At the time I'm writing, it's TikTok. But here's my opinion on some of these platforms and whether you use them or not.

Think of a social media platform dominated by the younger demographic as a nightclub. All the youngsters are there, hanging out with each other, listening to loud music, drinking, and having fun. They are not there searching for wedding venue information, right? Now, if you can show up at the nightclub with them, hang out, have fun too, awesome. And if the conversation happens to turn to, "Hey, what do you do?" Well, by all means, play it cool and tell them. And if all goes well, they might remember you later.

However, if you act like that guy at the bar trying to get your number who won't take no for an answer, your presence is going to blow up in your face. On the other hand, you also don't want to be the obvious "old person" trying too hard to fit in. That's not a pretty impression either.

I'm trying to make the point that if you don't go to nightclubs and enjoy it in real life, you won't do it, right? So, same with trendy social media apps. Just because your demographic hangs out there doesn't mean you have to too.

Not every app is meant to be used to push your business in someone else's face.

So, if you don't love new trendy apps, you have my permission to ignore them. However, you don't have my permission to neglect Instagram, Facebook, and Pinterest because you don't use them personally. If social media is a stretch for you, well, start warming up because it's a major place to build awareness with couples. They are using them on their Buyer's Journey to find you. Don't let them down.

I get that the struggle most people have with these platforms is what to publish. So, the big key with social media is what I call "constant, gentle pressure." That is having a consistent content plan for when you post and what you say. For example, posts on Instagram and Facebook could be about the weddings you have or the couples you are meeting for tours on weekends.

On Thursdays, which are "Throwback Thursdays," you could post a picture of the property from before it was a venue. Or a throwback to your wedding. Or something like that. Maybe Fridays are tips. Whatever you want to do. The point is that social media works best when it's active. And having a content plan ahead of time helps take the pressure of what to post and when.

I will sit down with venues I coach and help them create a content plan; I start by looking at a 12-month calendar. We go month by month, highlighting important times for the wedding industry, like Engagement Season, for example, and identify key holidays. Then we brainstorm ideas for posts during that time that we know will help a couple who is venue hunting decide to book a tour.

Also, knowing what couples are doing throughout the year as they plan for a wedding is helpful. After all, you can keep them engaged on your content because you deliver the right messages at the right times. I will touch on an advanced version of this when I talk about websites because you can amplify your reach with blogging on your site.

But when you sit down and break 12 months apart into monthly bites, you can quickly come up with some ideas of what you want your posts to focus on, and then it gives some work to do to find the right photos to use.

Organization and planning – remember that is a big skill for entrepreneurs. And with social media, if you sit down and do leg work ahead of time, you might find that you can be your own social media content manager pretty easily because the platforms all let you schedule posts ahead of time.

I will say that some of the most successful and highly engaging posts were when I posted a quick picture and few sentences about each couple that booked. When they signed the agreement, I would take a picture of them, tell everyone what day they picked, and a few items about them. And I welcomed them to our "family." It was like welcoming them to the secret club the venues represented.

This demonstrated publicly who our followers were and what they are like. It also verified and built trust with those who might be thinking of doing business with us but are not sure yet. And it also lets people know that the dates are filling up, so if you're waiting around, don't! And those elements are critical parts of effective marketing and selling strategy, which I will cover in the next chapter.

Creating Awareness with Vendors

Now, the second major way to build awareness in your early days is by getting on the radar of the local wedding vendor community. Because, since they are the seasoned and experienced pros that you aren't yet, they influence couples looking to them to make recommendations. What's cool about this process is that you are likely to meet new people and make many new friends. My best friend and editor of this book is a woman I met this way while in the wedding industry.

First, Join Networking Groups: Organizations such as the Wedding Network USA or the National Association for Catering and Events (NACE) all have local chapters around the country and host regular monthly or bi-monthly meetings. At these events, you will meet professionals in the wedding industry who can be great referrals for you.

Also, you will meet other venue owners, who are also a great resource. While many people think other venues are the "enemy," competition is not warfare. When venue owners realize that having several clustered together grows the market better than being the only one in your town, it opens many opportunities for everyone to benefit. As a result of this thinking, some communities have even developed their wedding-specific networking groups with city and county economic teams. Take a few minutes to go online and search for these in your area.

As I mentioned in the last section, you can also use Facebook to search for Groups to find other, wedding-centric people like you. Another upside to joining networking groups is that they typically have the meetings at venues the members own. So, this gives you a chance to surveil your competitors and take your turn to host a meeting at your location and let everyone see it.

Next, start direct marketing to Planners. Professional wedding and event planners exist in all communities, even if the companies specialize in more than one type of event. If you want to get the word out quickly, then reach out to all of them directly. Call them or send an email. Planners love to know about new locations because that insider knowledge helps them provide value to their clients.

Also, start direct marketing to Caterers. Catering businesses without their venues are great outlets to help you spread the word about your new venue. Think about this: you are creating more opportunities for caterers who don't have a property and are maybe prohibited from working at others with exclusive catering contracts. Therefore, they are always excited about a new location because that means more business for them.

Then, once your venue is ready to show off, host Trade-Only Open Houses. Once you've told everyone about your amazing new location, then schedule and host one or a series of Trade-Only Open Houses. Your guest should include wedding planners, caterers, bakers, rental outfits, photographers, and DJs. When you are brand new, I would expect your Trade Only premier to be popular. On these occasions, you have the stage and all the attention. Prepare an interesting presentation of your venue and provide everyone with an extensive tour. Also, be ready to hear their feedback if they have suggestions for improvements. They are the experienced pros in the industry – you may not be.

Finally, here's one of my favorites - offer free use of the venue for Styled Shoots. This is a fantastic strategy for creating awareness. To employ this one, reach out to local wedding photographers and let them know that they can do "styled shoots" at your location for free.

A styled shoot is when a group of wedding professionals such as bakers, planners, rental companies, wedding attire retailers, and a photographer get together and do a mini mock-up of a wedding. Typically, models are hired to play the part of the couple for the photos, and the photos from the styled shoot are submitted for publication in print or online magazines. Or sometimes, the photos are used by the vendors for their advertising. Styled shoots are ways for vendors to showcase their talents and skills more creatively than they sometimes get to in real life. As a result, these photos are the backbone of giving couples inspiring ideas for their events.

When you donate your venue to these shoots, your venue will get credit for the location and be mentioned in the publications and the rest of the vendors. Now, some venues charge for the use of the venue for style shoots, but I have found that the great, free marketing our venues receive far outweighs any of the money I might have made if I charged for it. Because the other payment to my venue came in the form of all the juicy photos, I got to use for my own business. Not to mention, by being a great venue to work with, rewards such as referrals come naturally. My client with 4,000 Instagram followers before ever hosting a wedding - this is what I told them to do, and the results speak for themselves.

My client is an example that you don't even need a finished venue to take advantage of this opportunity. I also did this with my farm during its renovation stages. The "incomplete" form of the venue can be an attractive backdrop all on its own. So, don't think again you need to be perfect to employ this strategy. Even if you're not ready to host a styled shoot, local photographers might be interested in the opportunity to use your property for other photos, like family or high school seniors. If you can work out a deal where you trade your venue for high-quality professional pictures, you have a bona fide win-win for you and the photographer. Plus, your name will start to work its way out into the community, and it will help with building anticipation for your opening.

Finally, once you start to host weddings, keep networking with new vendors at the weddings on your property. Despite networking at group meetings and reaching out directly to some of the professionals in your area, you simply will not meet everyone in the industry. So, when you do start to host weddings at your property, make it a point to introduce yourself to the vendors your couple has hired. And do your best to provide them with a positive experience at your location. You could even ask them for tips on how you can make it better for them, and you may learn some useful information. It's always important to make a good first impression on everyone in this business.

Before we end, let's talk about the other "old school" awareness marketing tactics of flyers, handouts, and other printed materials. I always say you should be cautious about investing in actual printed materials. That is because experience, research, and conversations with couples have taught me that most people these days don't find out about venues from flyers but online research.

Also, as a new business, you really can't afford to waste money on needless expenses, especially since the marketing tactics I've already listed are almost all free to do. With that said, there is a small place for printed materials in the venue world

Business Cards. I recommend you print business cards and have them with you, ready to hand out wherever you go. You will hand these out at networking meetings every time you meet a new vendor or bump into an engaged couple. They are a bit old-fashioned but still relevant. Fortunately, you can spend $20 and get 500 cards which will last you a long time, so this isn't a huge investment on your part.

Flyers or Rack Cards. Flyers or rack cards are great to hand out to couples during tours so that they have something specific to remember you by. Also, you can send them to local planners, caterers, and photographers to hand out to prospective clients– but ask them first if they want them! Also, your local Chamber of Commerce or visitors center may have a display rack that you could put your rack cards in, hence the name. These materials should list your venue website or phone number, plus your venue's key features. I would also add a few nice photos. I would not, however, put any pricing on there because if you change pricing each year, these will become obsolete fast.

Now, I also created a digital flyer because I noticed people doing the same thing I did at tours or events, which was, instead of grabbing the paper, they used their cell phone to take a picture instead. So, I created a flyer that had a QR code linked to our website. Then I put it in an acrylic display and set it on a countertop or table. I love this idea because it's paper-saving, time-saving, cost-saving, and yet does what you want it to do – gives someone something to take with them to refer to later. And when they don't need it, it goes into a digital trash can, not a real one.

Also, graphic design is not a skill most people have for marketing overall, whether it's your rack cards or designing cool social media posts. Still, today there are amazing ways to shortcut this shortcoming. I still use a program called Canva for all of my business graphics, but there are other similar types like Snappa and Easel.y, and I'm others will continue to come and go in the upcoming years. These online, cloud-based platforms all have templates ready to go, built for all uses, from social media posts to flyers to newsletters. Once upon a time, you needed to have some high-level graphics skills to create cool content, but now, it's much easier for the average entrepreneur to do it on their own.

So, do you remember what I said at the start about the personality facets that suit this business best? Well, if you love meeting people, developing relationships, investigating possibilities, this is the business for you. And raising awareness of who you are is where you will shine. So now that your couples know you are out there ready to do business with them let's turn that couple into a buyer.

14
GETTING A COUPLE TO SAY, "I DO" TO YOU

Okay – here we are on the couple's journey from first, getting engaged and starting their research into planning weddings and selecting venues, to now considering if your venue is one of their choices and making their decision on where to book.

So, if you got your name out there through all the tactics I went over on awareness building, your website and social media accounts are getting views. But we still want them to like you enough to get the emails and phone calls coming as well because those are a good sign that you have made it to the couple's shortlist of venue choices.

Making It Out of the Consideration Stage

In the consideration phase, your couple is figuring out what kind of wedding they want, what is important to them in terms of the venue they choose, and they are starting to make a list of places to visit that match these criteria.

And one of the places they looked to see if you make a list is your website. 0% of the couples I have met never looked at my website before contacting me—0%. So, if everyone looks at your website first, it makes sense that it needs to be done well since it's the first impression most people will have of you.

Think about how you use the internet. What do you think when you see a website for a business that is obviously out of date? You begin to form some not-so-flattering opinions about them, right? Also, have you ever gotten frustrated when you can't find what you are looking for because the navigation is confusing? Finally, I know I get miffed when I'm looking for information, and it's obvious that to get it, I have to call the company to find out. Honestly, I despise being baited into calling to speak to a salesperson because that just screams "high-pressure sales tactics," so I usually won't. Because I assume if you have to use high-pressure sales, your services or products just aren't going to measure up to what you're charging.

Now, did any of those feelings I just ran through sound like good marketing outcomes to you? Nope. So, I will repeat myself here: for god's sake, people, make it easy for your couples to want to do business with you! And the biggest and easiest way to do that is by impressing them right at the beginning with your website.

To quickly recap, through their initial research and planning in the awareness stage, the couple will narrow down to a type of venue they want for their wedding, like indoors or outdoors. And then, they will select some finalists based on the main features they think they need because they read a bunch of articles online about how to choose a venue. Or they will be looking for a venue with something they want, like allowing them to have their English Bulldog as a ring bearer.

So, if you don't have the information they are looking for on your website already in a clear, easy-to-find way, one of two things will happen. You will get a lot of emails or phone calls, all asking the same questions that you will have to answer over and over again. Or they pass you over for a venue with the answers they are looking for to simplify their search and decision-making process.

Remember in the market differentiation chapter where I talked about sometimes we have fears that a business will be difficult to work with, and we try to avoid that? That's what happens when your website isn't useful or clear. Now, back in the old days, it used to be hard and expensive to build a website, so there are so many outdated sites floating around the internet. But now, it's too easy to have one built for a relatively low cost, or you can make one yourself, with simple-to-use website builder platforms like Wix or Squarespace.

Today, having a bad website is just bad business. And further, most searches today are done on mobile devices, which is problematic for a business with an outdated website that isn't compatible with smartphone viewing. That's why along with my business consulting services, I also offered website design. And over the years, many couples have told me that they appreciated how well I designed my venues' website and that it was a major factor in them reaching out to me. So, here's what a high-converting wedding venue website should have:

Features. List out what your venue rental includes. Describe what you offer and make a point to state what your unique offerings are. Do you include chairs and tables? If so, how many? Features, like your Ceremony area, Reception Tent, Changing Rooms, etc., should all be described in words for SEO and shown in attractive pictures.

Key Policies: What is your catering policy? What is the length of the venue rental period? What is your alcohol policy? Hint: Those three questions are the top ones most couples have. So, if you can answer those and others like that on your website, the fewer you'll have to deal with later and the more likely it is that someone will book with you quickly.

Pricing. I believe that having your pricing online is a good decision. Some venues act more like expensive restaurants by not posting any pricing information because they want to make a couple travel to the property and then find out. Others are afraid that the competition will know what they are charging. Who cares? It doesn't matter if they know or not. Don't worry about them. Worry about your couples and their experience because a lack of pricing on your website has two negative side effects.

Someone may assume the "if you have to ask, then you can't afford it" rule and not bother with you. While others will call you or send an email and ask before taking the time out of their day to come to see you, so you're going to tell them anyways before a tour is scheduled. Why? The price matters! In fact, during the consideration stage, the price is a big factor since wedding budgets are usually pre-determined.

In the end, I don't believe in wasting anyone's time, including my own. So, having your pricing posted online allows couples to quickly determine if you fit their budget or you don't. If not, they aren't going to call you and take up your time with a tour. If you do, you've passed the first test, and now you know you have a better chance of closing the sale when you meet them.

Available Dates. The other big consideration question a couple has is if you are open on their date. That's why again, make it easy to do business with you and just show everyone your calendar. You'll need moderate computer and website-building skills to integrate a live calendar, but in my opinion, it's another valuable marketing tool. An online calendar tells a couple right away if their date is available at your location. However, a secondary marketing benefit is that a full booking calendar online creates a sense of urgency for a couple to hurry up and visit you because they might lose their date. As a new venue, an open calendar could look scary, but if paired with marketing content emphasizing that you are brand new, it puts it in the right context. On the other hand, an established venue with open dates is far more concerning because then I wonder what's wrong.

History or Story About Your Business. This is where you get to introduce your story of who you are and what you stand for. So have a page that shows pictures of yourself and accompany them with a nice, personal statement. This content tells your virtual visitors that, behind this amazing venue, there is a caring human being who has their best interests at heart. People love stories and personal touches; they bridge the gap between strangers, and in the next section, I'll explain why this is important.

Testimonials. We will dig in more about how important this is to have on your website, even if you're new to the business. This section doesn't have to include every review you've ever gotten. Having three nicely written reviews or testimonials is enough for a couple to see and read. I usually make these a simple strip on the Home page, right above the contact info. You could also put them right at the top, so it's the first thing couples see. That would make a great first impression, right?

Contact Info. This is the whole point of the entire website – to get the couple to contact you to schedule a tour. With mobile-oriented websites becoming more commonplace, the best place for your contact info is in the footer, so it shows up every page. This is also good practice because, during an internet search, you don't know what page on your site will show up in the search results. So, by having your contact info in the footer, it doesn't matter. Once your couple scrolls to the bottom of the page, they can click a button right there to send you an email or call you.

Blog. Now, I'm a writer, so it's easy for me to love blogs. However, I am also a human, so I know it's hard to stay up on one. But, from a strategic point of view, they are a golden way for creating great content on your website and generating views, so making time to do one is important. That is because as search engines index websites for future access during your couple's search, one of the criteria they use is how active a website source is. In other words, if you have a website that has the keywords in a search phrase but hasn't been touched in a few years, you might be ranked lower in the search results against a website with the same relevant keywords but has more recent activity. Search engines "think" that a more current website means more up-to-date answers to the search question. And search engines want to be useful to internet searchers. Make sense?

138

So, the easiest way to combine the one-two punch of keywords and activity is through a blog. A wedding venue blog that inspires couples should feature about 80% of the time articles of real weddings at your venue, with high-quality pictures taken by the couple's photographer. Then you should fill the article with website backlinks to the vendors who worked the wedding.

A blog also raise your page ranking during searches. So for the other 20% of the time, think of useful tips or policy information that current and potential couples might be interested in. To do a blog successfully means consistency and planning. And you don't need to publish weekly to gain the benefits. If you can plan on once a month and stick to it to start with you, you'll see great results.

More Photos, Less Text. Don't be shy about putting information on your website, especially your keywords. However, don't make it too text-heavy. A wedding is a visual experience. You want a couple to live vicariously through photos of other couples who have already been married at your venue. Shots of what the couple "sees" from the Head Table, Ceremony area, and picturesque vistas are valuable marketing tools. In this way, searching couples can more easily imagine their wedding at your location. Remember, even before you have weddings, you can get cool photos by collaborating with the photographers in your community, so don't fret if you haven't hosted a wedding yet.

Winning the Decision Stage

Okay, now you've made it to stage three of the Buyer's Journey: The Decision. And the work switches from educating the couple about you and your venue to motivating the couple to pick you over everyone else. And despite what you think, in the end, that decision will have little to do with facts and features. In my years, I have seen couples give up on a few of their checklist items to go with a venue that has something extra that just tells them that place is the place for them. Now, sometimes it is about facts – like you don't have the date they have to have, but even when that happens, it didn't mean the couple was happy about the decision.

So, what I'm about to tell you is the biggest opportunity or the biggest misstep all businesses make when it comes to marketing and sales.

ALL your branding, ALL your social media posts, ALL the conversations you have with couples, in person, on the phone, or in an email, ALL the copy on your website, ALL the pictures you post on Instagram, EVERYTHING

you share about you and your venue must create one or all of the three feelings in your couple to persuade them to book you.
1. Trust
2. Belonging
3. Fear

Yes, you can worry about Facebook's latest algorithms or if you should join TikTok or not, but none of that is as important as what I'm about to tell you. This is foundational stuff that is tried and true and time-tested. The how you get the messages to people has changed over the years, as we've discussed, but what you say and why you say it has not. And that's because we are all still humans, and we are tirelessly yet thankfully predictable.

So, let's start with **trust**. This feeling is centered on your reputation and your reliability. If a couple is fearful of spending a great deal of money with you or concerned that you will go out of business before their wedding or anything like that, the couple won't book, even if you have their date and no one else does. This means you must give them reasons and evidence to show you are trustworthy.

A major way is through testimonials or reviews. So, in your early days, ask your couples, their friends, and their family to leave reviews on the wedding websites and your Facebook page. Also, ask your first few couples to provide testimonials about why they picked you, even though you are new, then you can use these testimonials on your website. Also, make sure to include photos of people using your space or talk about the new people booking with you. Those are other forms of evidence that other people trust you.

There is an old belief that you don't want to have people in photos of building spaces. Well, sorry, the evidence is clear that when people look at websites or photos, the first places their eyes go are into the people's eyes in the picture. So, when your social media and website images show people in them, especially happy smiling people, a person viewing that photo will also feel happy thanks to a limbic synchrony feature in our brains. And if we can see the faces of people and look them in the eyes, and if we feel safe with them, our brains signal our bodies to release oxytocin – the trust hormone. It's science, people.

Trust also comes from whether you engage with the couple in a way that they feel like they can trust you. Do you look them in the eyes when you meet and speak with them? Do you smile? Does it look like you enjoy what you're doing? Are you confident when you answer their questions about how your venue operates? Or do you appear inconsistent or unsure? It's okay to say,

"Wow, I haven't been asked that yet. I don't know but let me find out and get back to you." But when you say that, do you get back to them?

Also, answering your phone and returning emails and phone calls consistently and timely lets the couple also know you're there when they need you. More about this later. Trust is letting the couple know they matter to you, their wedding matters to you, and you're not going to let them down.

So, in what other ways can you inspire or create trust with couples? Think about social media content you can post. Can you tell a story on your blog about a time you came through during a difficult situation? It doesn't even have to be about weddings if you are completely new. In fact, without hosting a single wedding yet, the only thing a couple has to determine if you are trustworthy or not is you and your personal experience. So, when you think about your story from the branding section, what might you talk about that would help build trust with people who have no idea who you are yet?

The next feeling a couple could have that would urge them to choose your venue over someone else's is a sense of **belonging**. In other words, they feel included and that your venue and business is something that they too want to be associated with. Either it's because they respect and admire the values you stand for, or when they see all of the happy faces of the couples at their weddings that have happened on your property, they feel like they are the same people and want the same things. This is our natural tendency as humans to gather in communities or herds with each other.

To build this sense and feeling of belonging means having your brand and the answer to the question "Who are we and what do we stand for," pretty well understood and communicated. The best ways to do this are again through your social media posts, the copy or words on your website, and in-person conversations and/or connections. Remember the exercise from the branding section about who your fans are and who they aren't? This is why we did that exercise. We are all wonderfully and beautifully different, and there is a community out there for everyone.

Talk about your community through your marketing work, and those who connect will want to join it. And again, if the couple feels like you "get them" more than the next venue - all things equal – they will book with you. Remember the couple that drove a long way to book with me because they felt like they belonged at our location?

So, again, what do the pictures that you post say? Who do they show? What values or behaviors are you communicating through your words and images?

Are they consistent? Is it clear what you stand for? Does what you say and how you say it really tell everyone why you are in your business and who your venue is perfect for?

Now the final feeling is the single most powerful motivator of all. It's the most primal feeling we all have because it's based on the only thing our brains are really wired to do – survive above all else. And so, the final reason a couple might choose to book with you, or not, is **fear.**

Building trust is, in a way, understanding that fear can push people away from you. So, you are trying to take away their fears by demonstrating that you are safe to do business with, right?

But the other things we fear, when it comes to business, are things you and I are pretty used to dealing with. For example, Black Friday sales and that you can get ridiculous discounts on things you want before they sell out. And the fear being played on is something called "scarcity," or the fear from limited money, time, or stuff.

And, not to sound creepy, but fortunately, the wedding venue industry is all about limited quantities. You have a fixed season with a fixed number of days you can host weddings, and that's it. The days you book is your limited inventory, and if you have a great summer, you can sell out your inventory. But if you do, you can't decide to "double production" because you can only rent out one day to one couple at a time. Plus, there are a fixed number of venues and vendors available to do weddings in your market, and when they book up, they are also no longer available.

So, one of the biggest motivators for a couple when booking their venue is to book quickly before they lose their date. Because once they have the date locked in, they now can go and lock in commitments from the other vendors for that date as well before they lose them too.

A wedding can't get planned and booked until there is a firm date. And most of the time, that hinges on the availability of a venue to host it. So, you don't have to act creepy to understand that fear is a huge part of businesses, particularly weddings. And there are not-so creepy ways to use this as a marketing and sales tactic for you.

For example, I have a sense of humor and like to have fun. So, when I wanted to let couples know that our calendar was filling up fast and that if they didn't hurry, we'd be sold out, I did it with humor and funny images or memes on Instagram. Plus, the more frequently I posted about dates filling, the greater the sense of fear of losing a date with us. It's like a snowball that keeps building momentum as it rolls downhill.

The other, more subtle way of letting couples know that your inventory is finite and selling up is by publishing your calendar on your website that shows what's open and what's not. And as your venue business grows, when couples push the arrow button to advance through your calendar and see all of the bookings already listed, it will give them a kick in the pants to get to you fast, or they will lose their date.

Now, back to sales or discounts – you can consider those too as a well to entice some bookings. I did some sales or discounts, like after a major wedding show for one week. But I rarely offered discounts on our venue because, to me, it sent a clear message that our venue was worth exactly what we're charging for it. On the other hand, having sales all the time implies that maybe you're over-pricing yourself and know it.

However, I got creative and chose to employ a variation on the scarcity fear. Because I changed our prices on January 1 every year – which happens to be right in the middle of Engagement Season – I would remind everyone that the new pricing will go into effect. If they want to book at the current price, they had until December 31 to lock it in. Again, I got the benefit from the fear of losing out *without lowering my price.*

To summarize this section, the point is that all of the messages you are sending out into the world, either directly or indirectly, need to create feelings of trust and belonging and hopefully eliminate a couple's fears about you and your business. And so, it's important to keep those in mind as you put everything together.

Wedding Venue Sales Activities

The final thing I want to talk about is your key sales activities and your sales team. Where marketing is getting one message to many people, sales is getting many messages to one person. So, marketing is everything you do during the Awareness stage and some of the Consideration stage. And sales are what you are doing in the Decision stage.

Your big moment in sales is when the couple comes out to your venue to see it and meet you, called the **Tour**. The tour is not just the chance to walk prospective clients around the property and let them see the fire pit, the place where the ceremony is held, and how big your tent is. Think of it as a walking presentation. During the tour, you have a chance to connect one-on-one with the couple on a more personal level. This is when you can sell your brand and build those feelings of trust and belonging.

Unfortunately, some people approach the Tour arms waving, "Here's the place. Got any questions?" and not as the awesome story-telling, brand-selling opportunity it is. And that is a huge mistake. I've heard from couples how venue owners or representatives appeared to be disinterested during the tour with the couple and how off-putting it felt to them. The couples left feeling like it had been an inconvenience to show them the space. You have to remember that this couple is excited to be doing this part of their wedding planning. And of all their choices in venues, you made their shortlist. So, don't forget to treat that choice with the respect it deserves.

Remember, it's about feelings. So, when your couple shows up, smile and congratulate them on their engagement. They are excited about that. Show them that you are excited about that too and the prospect of being the site of one of the most important days in their lives. Again, don't forget what kind of business you are running – you are going to be a part of dozens and dozens of weddings. Being at a wedding will feel like "no big deal" because it's your job, not a special event. But for your couples? This is a very big deal to them. Your memories of this business will include many different couples, but their memory of their wedding day will include only you --the place where it all happened.

So, when showing a couple your space, paint a visual of a wedding for them – how the chairs are set up, where the best places for sunset photos are, where does the wedding party goes when the ceremony is over. Make them a part of the conversation, "How do you see your idea of a s'mores bar in here?" "What kind of décor would you be using?" Help your couple "see" their wedding at your venue. Each step they take towards psychologically connecting your place by visualizing their wedding at your venue is one step closer to them signing the contract. This tour means serious money, so prepare for it.

That's why I highly suggest that you create a **sales script** for your tours. Much like a play, this script will layout the order in which you show the venue and provides what to say at each juncture. Don't read from it while giving a tour but commit it to memory and use it. The biggest value of a script is that it ensures that you, or anyone helping you, deliver a consistent message and cover all the important points during the tour.

But it's also a very big part of the branding of your venue because of the power of storytelling that I talked about in Chapter 10. During the Tour, you can walk your couple through why you chose to do things a certain way, where the inspiration came from, or history like "The bell here is the dinner bell from Keith's family farm down the road." Or "This barn was built in the 1940s after the original one burned down." Or "When it's not wedding season, we sit here too by the fire and enjoy the views."

Every tour I did was almost word-for-word, step-by-step, identical to the previous one. But, because I'd done them so many times, the script was delivered very naturally. However, I would evolve it as needed, like noting what things I say to get a laugh and what places I needed to sharpen. And I picked the right parts in the story to weave in key policies, so there weren't any misunderstandings or confusion later.

Another major sales tactic is hosting **regular open houses**. Every Wednesday night, from 6-8 pm in the summer only, I would open the venue doors at both locations for Open Houses. During this time, prospective couples were welcome to visit the properties and see the place at their leisure or get a tour. Also, our current clients who had already booked used this access for planning and walking through their wedding. While it was convenient for our clients to have this time to work and ask me questions, I found it also had other benefits.

The biggest one was when prospective couples came out to the venue and saw many other people on the site; it showed how popular we were. This then built those important feelings of trust and belonging. Plus, the Open House helps with the problem during the summers of not being able to do weekend tours since I had weddings happening.

Finally, you and your venue are the best sales team you have at the end of the day. Therefore, it's important to be mindful of keeping the property clean and tidy as best as you can. Also, make sure that anyone on the property is always professional and friendly towards visitors. I mentioned earlier the problem with rude and disinterested owners. So don't forget that everyone who works for you is expected to be friendly when a couple is there.

Sales, as many people learn, is a true art form. That's why it's important to think about who will be in this role for your business. It is the final, make or break step for you and booking a wedding. So, if you are not comfortable with being the key salesperson, you might have to hire the position out or encourage a family member to expand their skills. It can be someone that earns a commission or percentage of each wedding they successfully book, or if you can afford it, put someone good on the payroll.

You also have to plan how you will train new salespeople to learn your sales strategy. Part of your brand is consistency and, to simplify delivering that message, it's easier to prepare job checklists and scripts for when you have to hire and train a new person.

Now, here's a little downside news about the wedding venue business: wedding sales do not fit into a 9-5 schedule. Most of your sales activities take place on evenings and weekends, so whoever does this has to be available to work during those periods. This means answering the phone, replying to emails in a timely fashion, and meeting couples. For this reason, many venue owners are the sales team. But if you are too busy or uninterested in keeping those hours, you will have to hire someone, or you will never get a booking. If you make it too difficult for people with full-time jobs to contact and come out and see you and your property, couples will simply move on.

And about that email. Get ready for me to hammer home one of the most successful sales tactics I've ever used for my wedding venues. I'm not kidding when I tell you that a large percentage of my sales were due to one simple act: I answered every email inquiry about a tour almost immediately, day or night.

To some people, it might seem extreme, but my venues' full booking calendar said otherwise. I had my emails delivered to my smartphone, and before I went to bed, I'd check-in to see if I'd gotten any inquiries, and I usually did. Why? Because couples are sitting around together, in the evening after work, checking out your website and others, doing all their consideration stage work. And I knew that they probably have sent out several emails to other venues. But I found, not surprisingly, I was always the first one to answer back.

And in that one act, hitting reply just minutes after they'd sent me an inquiry, and saying, "I'd love to show the place! What day and time were you thinking?" was I how I earn that very powerful feeling of trust with couples right from day one.

Plus, if I'm the first to answer, I'm the first one to show them a venue. And by the time the couple makes it to my property and visit, the other venues haven't even answered their emails. Now, I'm closing the sale and booking them at my venue. It's that simple. And I have heard it from couples themselves about venues that take days (or never at all) to answer a request for a tour. It makes no sense to me because a swift, polite, and friendly response literally can make you money.

And once they book with you, don't stop. When the couple sends you an email with questions, answer them as soon as you can. And that doesn't mean in several days but one day or less. Showing them attention after they've booked with you reinforces that you care about their experience. And this, in turn, reinforces the other powerful feeling of belonging. We take care of our friends, and we ignore strangers.

Then a weird thing happens when you gain the trust and respect of your couple -- you establish a great reputation for yourself. And based on that, your couples will let their other friends know about it, and now you've unlocked the most valuable and cheapest form of advertising: *word-of-mouth*. And referrals or testimonials from your existing couples are like hiring new And salespeople – only you don't have to pay them! Happy couples will sing your praises to everyone they know, and you'll get more business as a result.

15
MANAGING WEDDING VENUE RISKS

Getting into the wedding venue business is certainly not for everyone in a myriad of ways. As I have mentioned several times over, there are many skills required for a venue owner to make the business successful. However, the other part of owning a venue business is realizing that you are opening your property up to be "party central" 20 to 30 times a summer.

Let me say that again. People think of weddings as only the ceremony. But the reality is that the ceremony and the lead-up to it is only about half to two-thirds of the entire rental period. Most weddings end with a two to three-hour, alcohol-infused, bass-thumping bash! And that's the point at which things can get sketchy and exhausting. So, to protect yourself from the uncertainty of working with humans, there are several steps for you to take ahead of time.

The Venue Rental Agreement

First and foremost, one of the most important tools for a wedding venue is your rental agreement. I'm going to give you an overview and start by saying I am not a lawyer. That means don't base your agreement on only my advice. I'm offering you key sections to include, and then I'm telling you to have your attorney review them and help draft a document that will solidly represent your business.

The reason why is this is a legal contract between you and the couple. A well-written agreement helps protect you against all the known risks you're going to encounter, including not getting paid! So, you want to make certain it captures the clauses and disclosures to protect you from some of the vulnerabilities I'll be covering.

Here are a few sections that you will want to include in your Agreement, as well as anything else your attorney recommends.

Payment. This section outlines how much the rental fee is, the payment plan option, and what happens if they don't make their payments on time. For example, we required a 25% non-refundable deposit to book the date. Then, the remaining balance was broken up into two equal payments. If the couple missed a payment, we could forfeit the agreement or cancel their date. And if they wanted to reinstate it, they had to make the missed payment plus a reinstatement fee of $200. Harsh huh? Well, guess what? I rarely got late payments.

Now, if a couple was having some financial issues, which can happen - I'm not heartless - I would find ways to work with them on coming up with an alternative, fair solutions. But if you don't start with the firm language in your agreement early on, you'll get strung along. You can be kind and understanding, but when some of your clients are immature, they forget that to get married, you have to be an adult, and adults have bills they have to pay on time. Plain and simple.

Some additional commentary about non-refundable deposits. It's the rule in the industry to take a non-refundable deposit to book a date. If you allow a couple their money back when they change their mind, you'll go broke. And if you don't take any money at all to book and only a couples' "word," you'll find yourself with an empty date on your calendar, which happened to me twice in my first season, before I learned my lesson.

A non-refundable deposit is skin in the game and makes the commitment real. I would tell couples that I charged the non-refundable deposit because they are buying a day on the calendar. And once I take the day off the calendar, any other couples who wanted that day see it's no longer available and move onto the next venue. So, I want to know that the couple is serious about buying that day and keeping it before taking it out of my inventory and giving it to them.

Now, if the day is put back onto the calendar, sometimes I could sell it again if it wasn't too late. But sometimes I couldn't, and that is not only lost revenue, but real costs already spent to cover a wedding I was no longer getting paid for. See, you must realize that for every day you sell on the calendar, you could do about five tours with prospective couples first. Plus, you will answer their emails, take their phone calls, and so on. The non-refundable deposit is essentially the salary needed to have someone do the work to book and serve a couple up to the wedding day.

Venue Usage. This section describes what the couple is getting and for how long of a period. It also describes the basic ground rules, covering noise, clean up, etc. And, it also has language in case the event runs over the venue rental period and triggers a penalty, which is usually an hourly fee. My advice in this section is to avoid specifics in describing what you are offering. Be clear but keep it simple. Specifics could get you trapped into being too inflexible if you must make a change, say in the manufacturer of tables you supply or the number of Shepherd's hooks you have.

Damage and Cleaning Deposit. Here you tell couples that they are responsible for paying a deposit, and it spells out the terms of getting it refunded, as well. It also covers what happens if the damages exceed the deposit. We'll come back to this in a bit.

Insurance Requirements. This section requires that the couple obtain Venue Liability Insurance and what the liability limits need to be. More later about this too.

Date Change or Cancellation Policy. This is a big deal and clearly defines what will happen to the contract and the couples' money if they change or cancel their date. We used to let people change their dates without a penalty. I did that only once. The first time I dealt with this issue, the bride kept changing her mind about what date she wanted, and every time she moved to a different day; I had to try to re-book it. Remember what I told you earlier in the non-refundable deposit section about the efforts into booking a day?

I learned quickly that not having a penalty spelled out made it too easy. So, I required a brand-new deposit for a new date. I also created a sliding scale on the venue rental refund by outlining key dates. If the cancellation occurs after them, they forfeit a portion of the venue fees already paid. This policy kept us from getting a last-minute cancellation, and then the couple expecting 75% of their money back when the proceeds of their rental fee were used to fund the preparations for their event.

Alcohol Usage. This part lays out the rules of the property, which are determined in part by State and Federal laws. You may elect to have additional restrictions on alcohol usage on the property. Some venues forbid hard alcohol and allow only beer, wine, and champagne. Other venues restrict how long alcohol can be served at an event. As I mentioned earier, my policy was that if you treat everyone like adults and set clear expectations for acceptable behavior and what isn't, you'll be fine. Bars and restaurants have been doing it for years.

Impossibility of Performance. This important section reminds the couple that the venue can't be held liable for certain circumstances that might cause their event to be canceled, such as acts of government, Mother Nature, or other causes like, oh I don't know pandemics and wildfires.

Decorations. Use this portion to describe what you will or won't allow on the property regarding decorations and how they're mounted or attached to your structures. If you don't want people nailing bunting around your gazebo or into your trees, tell them. Oh, and you might want to ban glitter, too, unless you want to see if you can use your vacuum on the lawn. Hint: you can't.

Now, there are several other subsections to a venue rental agreement that your lawyer will assist with since they pertain to indemnification, mediation, and other of the legalese that contracts should all have. So, spend some time and thought putting this together before you open for business. And then plan to revisit it and update it when laws, circumstances, or your plans change.

Other Risks

Even with a well-written rental agreement, you still have other risks associated with this business that I want you to be aware of. Some of these are related to your property, and some are related to your people. But for the most part, many can be reduced dramatically if you do some legwork ahead of time. Here's a list of the big ones to watch out for.

Implied Contract or Performance. Implied Contract or Performance means showing or telling customers things you have or what you will do for them if they book your location, even if it's not in the actual contract. The problem happens if you don't follow through on what you say, you have broken that "implied" contract.

For example, if you tell all of your prospective couples that by the time their wedding date arrives, you will have a brand new changing room built for them, and then don't; they will be upset. Or, if you do a tour with a couple and the tent has beautiful drapes and crystal chandeliers that you have borrowed just for show, if you don't tell them they are not included with the rental, they may assume they are. That becomes a real problem for you if they say those details influenced their decision to book with you, and then they show up in a naked tent.

Ultimately, the risk to you is that you have taken someone's money, and they assumed that they were getting something for that money based on your actions, conduct, or words. If you don't follow through or have some corresponding action to address it, you might be sued, or they may demand a partial refund of their rental fee.

So, what can you do to keep yourself out of trouble here? First and foremost, document in writing what is included with your venue and put it online where everyone can easily see it. Also, clearly state on tours what is included and what is not included with your venue rental package. That's why having a pre-prepared script that anyone who will be hosting the tour follows. It helps ensure consistency in what every couple is being told and eliminates misunderstandings.

If you are in the renovation stages of your venue business and booking for the following season, communication is important. Be transparent and communicate early if something important changes in your construction schedule; for example, the permitting process stalls the completion of the changing room. Be ready with a reason for the change and describe any remedies you have, like a replacement option or refund, before your couple demands it from you.

Finally, unless you plan on offering decorations, resist the urge to add them to dress up the property when showing it. Only have what it is you will provide and leave the frills out. Couples visit many venues with many different policies, so, naturally, they will mix up the details between their tours. That's why it's best not to do it at all. Your photos will show them what the space looks like, and that will be good enough.

Property Damages and/or Theft. Each summer, we would have about 6,000 to 10,000 visitors come through both locations. That's a lot of people with commensurate potential for inevitable accidents or wrong-doing. We've had cars and out-buildings broken into, chairs damaged, tables crushed, so on and so forth. You can't stop it, even with a chaperone on-site always, but you can keep it from bankrupting you.

The best tool for preventing damage is to take a Damage and Cleaning Deposit. Very much like the security deposit you put down on an apartment, this refundable deposit allows for small repairs to be covered quickly. But more importantly, it places the obligation onto the couple to do their best to make sure the property is returned to you at the end of the night the way it should be. When setting how much you are going to require, you want to make sure the value of the deposit is significant enough for people not to want to ignore it. In other words, it's gotta hurt if they lose it, which is why I suggest no less than $500.

Now, don't make the damage deposit another "revenue stream" for your venue. Meaning, don't go looking for ways to keep the money. Remember what I said about building trust with couples? Reserve it for emergencies only, remembering that wear and tear will come with the territory. So, every scratch and nick can't be a reason to keep someone's hard-earned dollars, especially after they've already paid you several thousand. Nothing leaves a bad taste in the mouth of your clients like tick-tacky deductions.

The few bucks you think you can pick up will be nothing compared to the lost weddings that result from a poor review. Instead, think of the deposit as the insurance premium you don't want them to pay; it will hit you in the wallet further on. I only deducted from the deposit when the damage was serious.

That meant 99% of the time, I returned 100% of the deposits at our venues. By setting clear expectations with the couple regarding behavior and conduct, plus having a chaperone on-site to keep an eye on things, I usually got what I wanted – my property back in my hands in the condition I rented it out. And the couples got what they wanted – their money back. That's a win-win situation and the way it should be.

Another tactic to help prevent property damage is to let other visitors at the wedding also know there's a damage and cleaning deposit placed. For example, when I meet with families and vendors at the rehearsal, I make a special point to tell everyone that the couple has paid a deposit and ask for their help with making sure the couple gets it back. I found that guests who act carelessly are simply unaware that their destructive actions will cost real money to the nice people who invited them to their wedding. Getting the wedding party, family and vendors involved means you've got more people invested in safeguarding your property, and it can vastly limit any issues or concerns.

Personal Injuries While on Property. Accidents happen, and they are unfortunate when they happen at a wedding. But even more unfortunate is that some individuals will take advantage of any situation. I'm talking about those people who love to sue or just threaten to. So, it bodes well for you to be extra vigilant about ensuring your property is safe for the general public.

Now trouble finds us one of two ways. It's either by surprise, or we went looking for it. And in the wedding venue business, that's also how people can get hurt. For the former, there are simple things you can do regularly when it comes to property maintenance to make sure that you have eliminated all the preventable ways a person may become injured. Those include:

- Get rid of or shield any exposed electrical wires or devices such as outlets without covers
- Eliminate or limit uneven terrain in high-traffic areas. If you can't, mark the spots with paint
- Before an event, inspect and remove any natural hazards like wasp and yellowjacket nests
- Have locked storage for hazardous materials such as fertilizers, gas, or other similar chemicals
- Put lights in problematic areas like the parking lot and make sure there is adequate lighting so that guests can see their way around perils in the dark
- Limb trees and cut down any that are hazards
- Place "No Trespassing" signs so that they're visible around the areas you don't want guests to go and consider adding locking gates or fences for prevention
- Have a First Aid Kit handy for minor injuries and bug bites

As for the latter, the trouble guests go looking for, that can be a bit trickier because to do this, you have to think about how to outsmart kids and drunk adults. And if you've ever tried to do either one of those, you know how hard that is. The first thing you need to do is minimize the "attractive nuisances" on your property. In tort or contract law, this is the doctrine that landowners can be held responsible for injuries to children who trespass if the injury is caused by an object on the property likely to attract children. This means that you make sure that any places where kids or guests will roam are safe or the hazards are known to parents. So, you need to think of anywhere on the property kids could wander off to and get into trouble, for example, ponds, barns or outbuildings, ruins or rocks, rivers, etc.

I made a point to alert parents to these areas and clearly inform them that they are off-limits during the rehearsal. The typical go-to of putting up "No Trespassing" signs doesn't work and won't legally cover you because small kids can't read. If you don't want kids to get hurt, it comes down to informing their parents. This is another reason for having a chaperone who can regularly patrol the property if these conditions are present to make sure no one is where they shouldn't be.

The other thing you want to do is to put away or garage all your equipment and vehicles. These are attractive climbing frames and "pretend" zones for kids, so ensure everything is safely secured. And this doesn't just apply to children. I have seen drunk adults attempting to start and drive one of our tractors left out in the back area, away from the reception.

Another simple but important thing is to keep anything you loan out in good condition. For example, make sure your ladders, dollies, and carts are sturdy and work. Plus, you want to make sure the chairs people sit on are not broken. And the chaperone should be keeping an eye on people trying to hang up decorations by standing on chairs and tables and tell them to stop. An ample supply of ladders in different sizes is convenient for weddings and great for preventing accidents and property damage.

Insurance

Aside from good maintenance and housekeeping, the biggest blanket of protection for you, your property, and your business are your insurance policies. Yes, that word is plural. At this time, you probably have health, homeowner's, auto, and maybe life insurance policies. Get ready to add some more. As I've mentioned, having a great small business lawyer and an accountant on speed dial is a must, you also need a really good insurance agent.

Some first-time home-based business owners make a costly assumption that their homeowner's policy is enough to cover any losses for their business. But your homeowner's policy is not sufficient for your wedding venue business. It's unlikely it will cover any injuries or damages that are related to the venture at all. Further, if you attempt to claim on your homeowner's policy for damages, and your insurance company finds out you have an undisclosed home-based business, they could cancel your policy altogether. This means you need to call your insurance agent and get yourself a business or **commercial liability and business property policy.**

A good, well-rounded business insurance policy can not only protect you and your property against the liability of someone hurting themselves during a wedding and trying to sue you, but it may also cover lost revenues. If, for example, you had a massive water main break and you were forced to close down for several months, your policy could cover the reimbursement of rental fees.

Known as business interruption coverage, this is extra to add to your policy for such threats, but you have to have already had it to benefit from it. Now, outside of global pandemics, huge factors can impact the business operations you want to be protected against. For example, what if a wildfire comes through and torches everything around you? Again, another very real concern for rural properties. With business interruption, not only would you have coverage to replace the buildings, but you would have coverage to replace the lost revenue.

A Little Extra: Venue Liability Insurance. We added a little extra icing on the insurance cake and required wedding or Venue Liability Insurance from our couples. This is a policy the couples purchase themselves for the day of the wedding. It provides coverage for the event host, the couple and the venue, against personal injury and property damage. The beauty is that it's the primary insurance for the event for covered claims; it will payout first before your business insurance policies kick in. In other words, it protects the venue from liability for the event itself, hence the name.

Several companies offer venue liability insurance just for the wedding industry, like WedSafe. They are usually more comprehensive and cost less for a couple to purchase than a rider on their own homeowner's or renter's insurance. The wedding-specific insurance companies also offer Host Liquor Liability, which we required the venue liability policy to have.

Host Liquor Liability is additional coverage that protects your couple and the venue from any injuries related to alcohol as well as property damage. This is really important for couples to understand that they could be held responsible for the actions of a drunk guest at their wedding who hurt themselves or someone else during or after the event, especially if that alcohol was given to them for free. That's why I made this a mandatory part of the event insurance coverage.

Insurance can seem tricky, which is why I highly recommend having a conversation with an insurance agent to work out the details and to get a quote. When you talk about the potential loss in revenue and the extra peace of mind, the couple of thousand dollars a year in paying for a business policy pales in comparison. And so, while there are risks to owning a venue, the truth is that preparation ahead of time dramatically decreases those risks. And being prepared allows you to have fun with this business instead of being stressed and worried.

16
PREPARING FOR THE BIG DAY AND MORE

We are in the home stretch finally, so let's fast forward to the future as you are getting ready to host the first weddings on your property. There are still a few more things you need to do ahead of time to be well prepared. One is to develop a few key guidelines and have them ready to share with your couples so their event and the whole experience go well. The other is to know what to do when, despite all your preparations, things don't go as smoothly as you hoped.

Develop Checklists and Guidelines

Before you start getting into the throes of wedding season, you will want to sit down and develop a written list of all the policies and guidelines the couples need to follow for the event. I recommend you keep this list handy and email copies to prospective clients and include them with payment reminders for your existing customers. I developed three practical resources for our couples for my venues that helped ensure everything would go smoothly during the wedding.

End of Night Clean-Up Procedures. This is a breakdown of what the couple is expected to do at the end of the night to satisfy your rules and ensure they get their damage and cleaning deposit back.

Include everything you expect and be as specific as possible so that there are no misunderstandings, for example, "Pick up all trash bags and place in Catering Prep area," or "If used for hanging decorations, remove all tape, fasteners, and strings from ceilings." Remember, you're dealing with varying levels of maturity and commonsense; the more descriptive you are, the fewer misunderstandings there will be. However, in my experience, two-thirds of the clean-up team at the end of the night are drunk, so complicated procedures are useless. Be clear and direct. And I suggest having the chaperone on hand to monitor and inspect the clean-up before letting anyone leave the property.

Because I placed such heavy emphasis on the Damage and Cleaning Deposit, the couple or their representatives did not want to leave until they were certain that they would get the entire balance back. Also, because of these clear end-of-event expectations, 99% of the time, the closeout of the event went smoothly, and I didn't have any problems.

Key Rules for the Venue. Your Key Rules are the fundamentals, such as where the designated smoking areas are or what your alcohol policy is, and your process for enforcing it. Make a big deal of getting these into the couple's hands before the event and urge them to share the details with their guests.

Also, you should back up your written guidelines with signage such as "Smoking Zone" and "No Smoking" decals where applicable. And, as your first line of property defense, if you are not going to be on the property during the wedding, then thoroughly prep your chaperone on the rules so that they become your best resource and monitor of behavior.

Diagrams and Dimensions for Floor & Space Planning. As soon as you have an idea of how your venue property will be laid out, I suggest you create some helpful planning diagrams of the property and key areas for the couples. If you hired an architect to help put together drawings for permits, these could be sufficient. But if you have other built-in features, such as an arbor that can be decorated, create a floor plan or diagram that shows the arbor's dimensions so that the couple can figure out how to decorate it. Also include key furnishing dimensions, if you are providing them, such as tables, tents, dance floor areas, etc. If you have a collection of diagrams to easily send out via email, it will save you from answering the same questions repeatedly. This is something I suggest you do before you begin booking your venue because these diagrams will be requested early on and could be good marketing collateral to send to prospective couples during their consideration stage.

Use the Rehearsal Wisely

Most wedding parties want to have a rehearsal before the event. Some couples opt to skip it altogether, while others conduct a rehearsal somewhere other than the venue.

We included a complimentary, 1-hour rehearsal period in our venue rental to be done during the week of their event. Sometimes couples chose not to use it, which was fine. And sometimes couples who didn't ask if they could add the hour to their rental, which I denied. I equated our rehearsal policy to a continental breakfast at a hotel – if you don't get your coffee and muffins in the morning when they are offered, you can't go to the check-in desk and ask for it at 10 pm. My policy was a "use it or lose it" system. You can choose to do it differently if you'd like.

Therefore, I recommend before you start doing sales work for wedding bookings, you first flesh out what your rehearsal policy will be. Will you charge extra for it or include it in the fee? How long of a period will you offer? Are you flexible enough to allow couples to rent extra time to have a rehearsal dinner on-site? What about time for pre-event set-up for a wedding on the following day?

Your answers to these questions will help shape your brand, the couple's experience, and the value you add to what you offer.

When the night of the rehearsal arrives, take it seriously. Through experience, I have found it is a great time to meet with the couple's inner circle and get buy-in on the venue policy and procedures. Ask for their help in enforcing them with the guests. You can also meet the representative from the wedding that will be "in charge" that day.

Because I believe in forming connections and wanting my couple to have their best day ever, I spent about 5-10 minutes welcoming everyone to the property at the very beginning of every rehearsal. At this time, I introduce myself, give an overview of basic policies and expectations, and then review the basic clean-up process.

I also asked for a show of hands of who is on the clean-up duty. Sometimes when I asked this question, I found that the clean-up team hadn't been figured out yet. If that was the case, I pre-empted a mess later because the couple has been put on point to organize their clean-up in advance. Otherwise, you could end with the chore yourself since no one else has stuck around to help. And, by gently coercing the couple into taking responsibility, they recover their damage and cleaning deposit—another win-win situation.

Tips for Handling Difficult Situations

Let's now talk about the other reason interpersonal, and leadership skills are necessary for the wedding venue business. Because sometimes, despite all your well-written policies, impeccable customer service, and on-point maintenance and landscaping, bad things happen.

I have mentioned the power of feelings and emotions several times in this book for a good reason. Weddings are emotional affairs, and they evoke extreme feelings. Unfortunately, not all the feelings are positive, especially as scattered friends and families gather and people vie for attention. During the planning process and the wedding, there is also stress and anxiety that can reveal itself in behaviors that might appear rude or inconsiderate.

And so, since we are all humans and no one is immune is from the spectrum of experiences and emotions that come with being one, it's best to just know where some triggers and land mines are and how, if possible, you can avoid them. The following is not all-encompassing, but it is a highlight reel of the common low lights of a wedding.

Bad Behaving or Upset Parents. Back in the day, I found that about half of our couples were paying for their wedding while the other half were getting financial help from parents or other family members. Unfortunately, this financial support sometimes came with strings attached, such as the "helpful" family member feeling entitled to have a place in the wedding planning process.

When a parent is excluded from a big decision like choosing the venue or bringing their own, often outdated or traditional assumptions about what a venue should be, conflict can arise. Sometimes this comes up during the weeks leading to the event, or sometimes it manifests on the wedding day.

The first thing to do with an upset parent or family member is to keep your cool and stay out of shouting matches. Breathe deeply and regularly while you suppress any defensive responses. Maintain your composure and speak in a regular tone at moderate volume.

Allow them to unload by clearly and fully communicating their concerns with you. If they have objections to your policies, just let them know that everyone has the same rules applied to them. Explain that each guideline has a practical reason behind it that protects all involved. You've tested and adapted these rules over time, and they work so far.

If they are just nit-picky about your venue, inhale and thank them for the feedback. And then ask yourself what is important: Being right or satisfying your clients? This business is an exercise in patience. You have to be the better person if you're going to get rave reviews.

I have had to watch a father of the bride leave the wedding, return home, and bring his rakes to the property. Then I watched him re-raked the bark flower beds to even it out and get every loose, dead leaf he could find. I also met the bride's mother, who asked me if we'd reconsider painting the house to a different color that would match the wedding better. No joke.

Sadly, I've seen narcissistic mothers of both brides and grooms creating any melodrama they could just so that they were the center of attention. And I've had to find my deep, deep internal reserves of diplomacy to not tell them to get their act together. Instead, I shifted focused on making sure the couple knew that it was still their day, and I was there to support them and see to it that they had a wonderful wedding. In the end, you owe your obligation to the people who signed the contract with you. And if it was the couple, then their opinion is the only one that matters.

Bad-Behaving Guests. Serving alcohol at weddings has its good and bad sides, as we all know. The downside is that it can turn very nice people into raving lunatics or, at least, idiots with very big chips on their shoulders. Add this to the social time bomb that's a mix of exes, new loves, bad breakups, and old jealousies, and you have the ingredients of a very interesting soap opera.

Believe it or not, back in the day, before getting into weddings, I spent about a year helping a community organizer with trying to clean up a problem tavern in a crime-ridden neighborhood. It was one of the best and scariest jobs I ever had. That environment taught me how to handle some pretty rough people. I could get them to do what I needed without getting myself, or anyone else hurt. Now, I will say that the worst thing I've ever dealt with at a wedding pales compared to what I dealt with in that bar, but handling the situations is similar.

The late comedian, George Carlin, once said, "Never argue with an idiot. They will only bring you down to their level and beat you with experience." I have found that this reasoning applies to drunks. So, a gentle approach is best when you have a rude guest to the wedding staff or other guests. I know that you may want to grab them by the collar and throw them out the door, but you have to remember that the wedding is a private event and if this person is there, they must have some special place in the lives of the couple, so treat them with respect.

The first thing you should do when dealing with an unruly guest is *don't*. Go straight to the person the couple has placed in charge, which could be a planner, family member, or friend. Then, let them know about the situation. In my experience, the people hosting the wedding, such as the couple and their family, always do the best job of keeping the guests in line because they have a personal connection. They can further restrain or tame the individual than you could, without the formal ramifications you could face.

If a guest is beyond reason and the family cannot manage the situation, you should work with them to decide if they need to leave. If you are ever in the position of having to speak directly with an unreasonable person, my advice is to take them aside, speak in a low, calm voice and be firm and direct. Try not to put them in a situation where they are being singled out and could feel attacked or embarrassed by the attention. This only intensifies the situation. And ultimately, if the guest is disruptive and there is a concern, it could take a violent turn, speak to the family, and make a unified decision to call the authorities.

Unsupervised Children. Second, only to drunks, unsupervised children are a big reason couples lose portions or all their damage deposits. When kids are forced to stay on the property all day long while their parents help with set-up, and they are then in the wedding, they can become extremely bored and destructive.

I found that children love to pick all of the flowers in the flower beds, destroy lawn games, use candles to light things on fire, and write on the walls. I have also found through the years, when you see kids doing something that will result in injury or damage, and you attempt to correct their behavior, you will get a "You're not my mom" response.

So, it was my policy to let a family know at the rehearsal and when I meet everyone on the day of the wedding that if children are seen doing something they shouldn't, I'll bring it directly to their or the attention of the person in charge to handle. And, if you do that enough times, they will get it and manage the situation on their own.

Cancellations and Refunds. Sadly, weddings do get called off. Sometimes the couple has decided to end the relationship, and other times, life has simply shifted a little, and their priorities or circumstances are different. In any case, handling a cancellation is not a straightforward process. And in 2020, well, weddings were especially hit, and couples who thought they were having a big, grand affair that summer were dealt a devastating blow.

Remember how your business accepts a non-refundable deposit to book a date? Well, when cancellation happens, you will find yourself questioned by the couple on just how non-refundable a non-refundable deposit *really* is. They will test you in emails, phone calls, and just when you are tired of repeating yourself, you'll get a call from a helpful family member like mom or dad. They'll want to show you how young the couple is and how they can't afford to lose that much money. Or how the bride-to-be's heart was shattered by that jerk, and not getting her money back is just adding insult to injury.

At this point, you must decide where your line in the sand is. Are you going to stand firm 100% of the time, or will you be willing to negotiate? In my business, I did a little of both.

No matter the circumstances, my first response was always to remind them that the contract was very clear and that the deposit was non-refundable. I reminded them that during the tour, I was very firm that the deposit would be non-refundable. And when I finally booked them, again, I reminded them that a non-refundable deposit means "You don't get it back even if you change your plans."

Sometimes, with the facts presented to them, the client understands, and the discussion is over. You should also note here how many times I did tell them about the terms of the deposit – because you don't want it to be a surprise or you have no legs to stand on.

If they press and you are willing to listen, after that, it's up to you to decide if you have sympathy for the circumstances and whether you can afford to return the deposit or not. Like I said, sometimes I did return it. I didn't have a hard, fast rule for when I did and didn't, but I am a human being, and sometimes I just got that feeling that it was the right thing to do.

How often will this happen to you? I can't say for certain, but at our venues, with two locations and about 60 to 70 events a summer, we got about 4 to 6 cancellations each season. So, it doesn't happen frequently, but it can be pretty taxing to deal with when it does.

Handling Your Own Mistakes

Now, what if you have to cancel a wedding or event because, let's say, your septic drain field fails, and you aren't allowed to host any events until it's fixed? That is a gut-sick feeling no one wants to deal with. Or you made a

163

mistake because you double booked a rehearsal or forgot an appointment, or the worst of the worst – you double-booked a wedding! Whatever the issue is, mistakes are common and learning how to handle them as a business owner is mandatory.

So, what is the magic formula for handling mistakes as a business owner? Well, I have four steps for handling the mistakes in business that will help maintain or restore the trust between you and your couple.

1. Own it. That's right. Own the mistake and do it quickly. The longer you wait to acknowledge you messed up, the longer you allow your couple to be upset, and a small problem can grow into a big problem. Want to know how to get a bad review? Make a mistake and then ignore the offended party. That will do it every time. But what if you find out there's a problem and you just don't know how to fix it yet? That's okay. Just don't ignore your customer's email or phone call. Just be honest and let them know you're going to figure it out. And then apologize and validate their discomfort because the sooner you can calm them down, the better the outcomes will be for everyone.

2. Now fix it. Figure out the remedy for the situation and stand by it. And accept the fact that mistakes are costly, so be prepared to pay whatever it takes. And try to avoid being cheap because it leaves a bad taste in your couples' mouths. No, you don't want to have to return the money, but sometimes it is truly the right way to fix the situation, whether you like it or not.

3. Don't do it again. I was willing to fix my mistakes quickly and fully because I could always tell myself, "Well, now we know that we are going to make sure that never happens again!" because after an error or mistake was made, I always figured out how to not repeat it. Sometimes mistakes are from a lack of proper maintenance, but mistakes often stem from misunderstandings and poor communication in the venue business. And so, to keep from making the same mistake, your corrective actions might just be to improve the wording on your website or marketing materials and make sure the venue is in better condition. Again, mistakes are common and expected, but repeating the same one is a sign of something much worse.

4. Don't quit. Again, there is nothing as heart-sinking as finding out something is wrong. And it is perfectly natural to want to quit just to avoid any future embarrassment or fear. But come on – are you really going to quit over one little mistake? No, of course not. So, get back out there and keep at it.

Truthfully, most weddings go smoothly with zero issues. And when there is something unforeseen, if you think of it as a learning experience, it helps put it into the proper perspective. Nothing in life is perfect, but having a plan or expectation ahead of time will certainly make you more confident and have as much fun as possible doing this business.

17
CREATING YOUR PLAN

Alright, here we are. You have just learned all the in's and out's of starting a wedding venue business on your property. But is that good enough? Nope. Because now you're probably thinking to yourself, "Cool. But how do I get all this done?" Fair question. So, in my re-do version of this book, I've added this chapter on planning, and I'm offering helpful tips for overcoming the nagging fears you will have as you get into being your own boss, maybe for the first time.

Setting Goals

To summarize the efforts involved with starting a wedding venue business, remember two sets of activities. One is the functional work of the business itself, like permitting, marketing, property maintenance, etc. Then there's the second, often overlooked set of work which is your personal development. And no matter how seasoned of an entrepreneur you may be, we always have room for growth.

When someone sets out to build their plan for their own business, they constantly forget that to achieve their professional and financial goals, they may also have to undergo some renovation work. For example, you might realize that overcoming your fear of speaking in public is an important thing to work on or that you realize that your confidence is causing you to constantly undervalue yourself.

Whatever the concerns are, when you set out to plan for how you will start this business and what you will do, I want you to keep those two buckets in mind: you and your business. And this looks like you, first laying out the business goals and then looking at them and asking yourself, "Okay, what do I need to improve in myself to be the kind of businessperson who can achieve and be successful at this point in the timeline?"

Now, when most people set goals for themselves, whether it's in business or personal like, "I want to lose 20 pounds," or "I want to save money to buy a car," they keep the goal too general for it to be effective. And so, most business experts, from coaches to managers, have learned that to set an effective goal, it is best to make it S.M.A.R.T.

So, for those of you who haven't heard of S.M.A.R.T. Goals, they are Specific, Measurable, Achievable, Relevant, and Time-Dependent. And the principle is that when you write out goals or milestones in your plans, you have the best chances of success if they are structured in the following way because they are easy to understand, follow-through, and you can verify if you've done it or not. Using this strategy also helps them become concrete because you aren't making them so generalized that you can't figure out what you are doing and why. Here's how you create them.

Make your goal Specific. This means you avoid general statements and say exactly what you want to do.

Make your goal Measurable. This means having a target or some metric to meet that helps you see whether you achieved it, like saving $5,000 instead of saving for a new car.

Make your goal Achievable. This is tricky but important because, what you are asking yourself as you develop your goals is, is this something you really can do? For example, if you start with a goal that requires more time, effort, or even money than you have, again, you are asking yourself to do something that is simply not possible at the moment. Not only is that unfair to yourself, but it also sets you up to fail even before you begin, which is self-sabotage in disguise and a real confidence-killer.

For example, with the venue business, you will not be able to earn everything you want in the first summer. In my experience, it will take 2-3 summers to build your name and get the bookings to the point you want. Why? Well, because weddings are planned 12-18 months in advance. So, you need to plan for that delay and set achievable goals for yourself so that you don't become demotivated quickly.

Make your goal Relevant. Again, when you set out to accomplish goals and tasks for yourself, you must constantly be asking if the work moves you towards your objective or away.

Make your goal Time-Dependent by having a deadline on it. If you don't set deadlines or durations, you have not made it urgent or important, and so then it won't be. Deadlines, as you know, also help hold us accountable for our choices. Some people hate deadlines because they don't want to pressure themselves or risk failing. When I set timelines, I don't say "in 3 months," but I put a real date on it to add realistic urgency to it.

Now, when it comes to deadlines, if I don't meet them, I don't judge myself, and you shouldn't either. Instead, I want you to use them as a part of the learning process. For example, if you estimated you would have your venue's permitting done by a certain date, and then you pass that date, ask yourself why. Did the work involved take longer than you realized because you've never done it before? Or were you trying to do too many things at once, and so the activities related to permitting sometimes got pushed aside for other things?

In the end, when you set a goal, making them time-dependent is not intended to set you up for punishing yourself. However, that does not mean they aren't important, and you shouldn't worry about sticking to them. They are milestones and necessary to stay on track towards your goals.

Finally, here's one last thing I always bring up in goal-setting exercises with clients, and that is, what is the point of these goals? I know that seems obvious, but we have to think of each goal we set as a link in a chain that has to connect to the next link. And so, when we think about what goal we are setting, we have to think about each goal's interconnectedness to the next goal we need to undertake and how they all link us to the overall outcome we are aiming for. Also, knowing the result we are aiming for allows us to re-evaluate our goals to see if they are still the right ones or if something has changed, either in our environment or the result we want, we may need to adjust.

So, then, an example of a S.M.A.R.T. Goal with a clear outcome is:

"To eventually make $80,000 in personal income per year (outcome), given my business expenses, I need a sales plan that ultimately generates at least $120,000 per summer in gross sales (specific and measurable.) I plan to start with sales targets of (10) bookings at $4,000 for the first summer we open, so the venue breaks even. Then, my target is at least (20) bookings or at least $80,000 in sales in the second summer. Finally, by the third summer, the target will be to hit $120,000 or approximately 28-30 bookings over four

months (specific, measurable, achievable, and time-dependent.)

With that example of a larger goal, you can now break it down into smaller sub-goals, which leads us to the next part of business planning which is organizing your plan by looking at the long, mid, and near-term objectives. And this process may be different than what you are used to because it's planning backward from where you want to end up to where you are today.

Step one is to pick a point out in the future for you and your business that is the end goal. How far in the future is up to you, but realistically, this is about five years out from your beginning point for a venue business. While that might seem long, a five-year timeline includes a couple of years of start-up and business growth and then ends with a year or two of operating at the lifestyle level you want.

Now, after you have that long-term vision out there, ask yourself how you will know you reached the halfway or mid-point? The easy answer is that it will be two and a half years from today. Wrong. What I mean is, what are the objectives, goals, and skills you need to have earned, achieved, or developed by the halfway mark? What features does your venue need by then? How many staff members will you have? What are your sales targets at the halfway point?

Finally, let's break down the halfway point in half also. These become what I call the near-term goals or objectives. So, think about the next 12 to 18 months. What do you need to be working on and have completed or achieved so that you are halfway to halfway, or 25-30% of your entire journey?

Are you really done yet? No, because now that we have the near-term set, we can break that down further into bite-sized monthly targets and mini-projects. So, you ask yourself, what does each month look like for the next 12-18 months so that you are on track? What are you starting and completing before you begin the next steps, and how will all these links together to get you to where you need to be to sit down one year from now and plan out the next 12-18 months?

I liken this process to using a road map for a road trip. You pick your destination and the day you are planning on arriving, and then you work backward, figuring how long it will take to drive and what pit-stops or overnighters you will have along the way.

The other important part of goal setting is to always check in with your progress. First, I look out long-term on the horizon and make sure that, yep, I am still heading in the correct direction. Even though I can't see it specifically, I know the destination is out there in front of me. I then put my head down just a little and review the route out ahead of places I haven't gotten to yet but will, and make sure that, yes, it still seems like the right way to go. Or sometimes I will ask myself, "Am I making good time here? Am I ahead of schedule, and if so, would I do something a little differently now?" like maybe moving up some other plans, like hiring staff sooner or adding that next cool feature. And then, I check my spreadsheet and some of the monthly targets and tasks I have there.

Sometimes you find, as time goes on, that you will need to adjust, and that's okay. Goal setting and project management need to have some flexibility built into your plan. But, the important thing is to be very clear and fixated on the destination and vision you have for the venue and yourself so that it becomes obvious to you what you work on and what you don't. Because if it's not going to get you where you want to go, or it needlessly slows you down, you will need to learn to become stingy with your time and your money and say "No" a lot more than you might do now.

Beating Your "What If's"

Alright, planning is great, but what if nothing goes according to plan? What if this isn't the right time to start a wedding business? What if this turns out to be harder than you thought? What if you never get any bookings?

Well, welcome to the scary world of entrepreneurship where danger lurks everywhere, especially in your head. Sure, there are real risks to owning your business, and we've covered many of them here in this book. But the real risks that seem too difficult to overcome are the ones we keep replaying in own mind, over and over again. So, I want to give you a strategy to use if you find yourself in one of these emotional traps that are causing you to doubt yourself and your abilities to reach your goals.

Step 1: Remember why you are doing this. Yes, the first step in this exercise is to fall in love all over again with your idea or goal. You do this by weighing the positives and negatives of pursuing it or staying on the current course. Go back to the reasons you put down on paper earlier and look at the Lifestyle Levels you created and remind yourself how utterly amazing it will be when you get there. And if you must, write those reasons down again so that you see them. Close your eyes, push away the doubts, and just let yourself feel a new life: the vacations, the mortgage paid off, the free time –

whatever it is you are trying to achieve.

Step 2: Now you're in the right frame of mind to list out the worst-case scenarios, one by one. While you put your fears into writing, you might start to feel your anxiety levels building back up. That's natural so, it's important to remind yourself as you do this that all you're doing is creating a simple, to-do list and don't go much further down the fear rabbit hole than that if you can. I also want you to do this exercise for your fears about doing this business as well. When you consider all the things that worry you, you might end up with a list of what-ifs that look like this:

- What if a wildfire torches the entire property, and I have to cancel weddings?
- What if someone hurts themselves while at a wedding and sues me?
- What if the County delays approving my permits and I can't open my venue on time?
- What if the estimates for the construction work are too high and I can't afford it?
- What if I don't get any bookings for the first year?

Step 3: After you've brainstormed all the things you are afraid of, next is to brainstorm ways to prevent them from happening because there are solutions to most of our problems or things we can control. And the best way to do this is to keep your thoughts carefree and confident, like, "Really? No bookings? As in zero? Honestly, that's really unlikely if I do the basic stuff I need to do to create awareness in the local industry."

Step 4: Finally, let's imagine that despite your efforts to control what you can, your what-if comes true anyway. Okay, then why not think ahead of what your Plan B is so that you have the comfort of knowing there is one? For example:

"If it did happen that I don't get a single booking my first year, it's obvious I would just need to make sure I have saved enough money before I quit my job to cover my major expenses for a year. So, I should make sure as I'm doing my start-up costs, I also write out every business and personal bill I'd have to pay out of my savings and have a separate savings goal just for that. And then when I hit that magic number, I know it's safe to quit my job and go full steam ahead with my business."

In my years, I have found that turning your fears into a to-do list is useful for planning anything from what tasks to do in your business and prepping for difficult conversations with other people. And I would not expect you to stop using something like this since we are all humans, and being afraid is as natural as breathing. But what you want to try to avoid is getting lost in replaying them in your heads. If you confront them and plan for your what-ifs, the benefit is two-fold because it allows you to be well prepared and will raise your confidence.

Putting It All into a Business Plan

Finally, some of you reading this may be in a position of needing a loan or some form of financing to get your business started. If that's the case, you will need to have a nice, well-written business plan to present to your bank or lender. Fortunately, we have covered in detail through this book all of the information you will need for this, so I'll just give you a breakdown of the sections.

As you complete each section, don't stress over lengthy paragraphs. Instead, think about this being an easy-to-read document. That means try to use bullet points where you can so that a person could skim through but still grasp what you are doing and see that you know what you're talking about.

If you aren't getting any financing or financial help, this activity is still valuable because it helps bring all the bits involved in creating this business together in an organized thought.

Company Description. Start by spelling out in one paragraph what you will do, what differentiates you from other venues, and the markets or couples you are proposing to serve. Think of this section as an elevator pitch that gets to the point but without the details. Those are coming.

Market Analysis. In this section, you will start getting a bit more detailed and let the reader know what you already know about the wedding market and why you think it needs another venue like yours. Also, write down what you assume or do know about the competitors in the market. And then describe the couple you are targeting. This information should come from your market research and branding activities.

Organization and Management. After looking at how a venue business operates, you know there are several specific job functions. In this section, list out who are in these roles when the business starts and write out your hiring plans for additional staff, with dates when you are planning for those hires. This section also clearly states who's in charge and how major decisions are made or divided between the key owners/managers. If you know how to create an **organizational chart** that shows the management and staffing in an easy-to-read visual, I'd recommend that. Most word processing applications have that feature in them, so it shouldn't be hard to include. In my plans, I would also include my brief bio and resume as an attachment to see my relevant personal experiences. This is key because you must demonstrate to a lender that you have qualifications to be the company owner, so they trust you enough to give you money.

Advisors and Specialists. Your bank or lender will also want to know that you have some experts on your team helping you. The obvious business specialists are attorneys, accountants, and insurance agents. But you could also include others here like your business coach or consultant, or maybe your freelance social media coordinator.

Venue Features and Services. This is where you take the general and get more detailed about what you are setting out to do and what your venue will offer. If you are going to open with an MVP version and then add on as income increases, spell that out here.

Marketing and Sales Plan. This is a great section for bullet points. You have already been shown a few ideas for creating awareness and getting couples to choose you, so document those here.

Financial Plan. This is another great section for bulleted lists of your anticipated start-up costs and what you have figured as your ongoing costs. Also, show the reader that you have broken out the cost of sales for the venue operations. As you can imagine, if there is anyone section of this business plan that will be of interest to a bank, it's this one. So, impress them with your homework.

In my plans, I also included a spreadsheet that showed the cash flow for the business and projections for sales. Again, at the end of the book, I will tell you how you can get your hands on a spreadsheet I've built that is handy for this section.

And there – now you have the draft of your wedding venue business plan. And now that's done, I want you to do yourself a favor and make a few calls.

First, phone your attorney. If the lawyer you have now does not specialize in business, ask them for a referral. Set up an appointment and sit down for an hour to review the plan and have them help you choose the right structure for your business. You might also go ahead and pay them a couple of hundred dollars for them to file the necessary business registration paperwork with the state and federal government. And, after you've met with them, do the same with your accountant. Have them review the plan for viability and reasonable goals.

What do I mean by a "structure?" Your business structure is the legal framework your business will operate under, like a corporation or LLC. It defines how the legal system and the government, particularly the IRS, will view you and your business's revenue. You want to set everything up the correct way from day one because the right structure will further protect you and your home from any liability or risk and provide you with the most favorable tax position.

18
CONCLUSION

Okay – you did it! You made it through this whole book! Do you know what I think you should do? I think you should give yourself a nice reward. Why? Because most people don't complete the books, they buy. They get started when they are excited, then become overwhelmed by the work they see is involved.

And normally, people do a couple of things – quit and never start or ignore the hard work because they see other people not doing it, and so they think that it's a completely acceptable alternative. And perhaps they assume that the instructor or author is just overly cautious and trying to give you busywork.

But since you read the whole book, you know better! And what you know is that 50% or more of all businesses that begin close. And the bottom 50% are the ones winging it and ignoring the work involved in avoiding the hazards of entrepreneurship. And the top 50% are the ones who do some of the key things I laid out in this book.

The top 50% are entrepreneurs who have a balance of financial know-how, organizational and planning skills, and leadership or people skills. And those who realize that they are weak in one or some of those know that they should be working to improve them.

The top 50% also realize that market research is a fundamental tool all businesses use to make smart decisions about how to run their venue business and provide exactly what their couples are looking for. The top 50%

don't guess. They research. And then use that research to create powerful and emotional branding, marketing, and sales strategy to get couples to book them.

Finally, the top 50% of businesses also know that being smart with money is critical. And that includes knowing how to price your venue so that you can pay yourself and give yourself the lifestyle you want.

I also hope the other big bit of knowledge you take away is the importance of a firm vision in your mind about the kind of venue business you want to create for yourself. Because, in the end, remembering why you are doing this all makes the hard and necessary work worth it.

Resources

To support your journey as you develop this business, I have several resources outside of the book that you may be interested in.

The big one is the **www.weddingvenuebiz.com** website I set up with a blog plus links to the online courses I offer to aspiring and actual wedding venue business owners. In the modules of these courses, I include checklists, handouts, and spreadsheets to help with the planning work. This is where you can find the financial spreadsheet I refer to a few times in this book.

I also write more generally about business and entrepreneurship through other books. So, if you like my writing style and want to get more in-depth with some of the topics here, I have a book called *The Fearless Woman's Guide to Starting a Business: What Every Woman Needs to Know to be a Courageous, Authentic, and Unstoppable Entrepreneur.*

In that book, I cover the challenges women, in particular, have in the world of entrepreneurship plus the knowledge and strategies to overcome them. Some of that I touched on in this book, but I go deeper in the other one. And I'm pretty proud of that book, too, if I say so myself.

And if you loved this book or even liked it slightly better than average, I would be grateful for a review if you bought from an online retailer. Reviews help others find the book, so if it helped you, a nice review would help someone else who's dreaming of doing this just like you.

Thank you!
-Ameé

REFERENCES

"Frequently asked questions about earnings data from the Current Population Survey (CPS)," U.S. Bureau of Labor Statistics, accessed March 15, 2020, https://www.bls.gov/cps/earnings-faqs.htm.

"Frequently Asked Questions About Small Business," U.S. Small Business Administration Office of Advocacy, September 2019, https://cdn.advocacy.sba.gov/wp-content/uploads/2019/09/24153946/Frequently-Asked-Questions-Small-Business-2019-1.pdf.

"Labor Force Statistics from the Current Population Survey," US. Bureau of Labor Statistics, accessed March 15, 2020, https://www.bls.gov/cps/cpsaat39.htm

"National Association of Catering Executives Survey: More Weddings, Bigger Budget," PR Newswire, April 13, 2011, https://www.prnewswire.com/news-releases/national-association-of-catering-executives-survey-more-weddings-bigger-budgets-119765579.html

"Newlywed Report 2020," https://go.weddingwire.com/newlywed-report

"The Knot 2019 Real Weddings Study," https://www.wedinsights.com/report/the-knot-real-weddings

Kim, W. Chan and Renee Maugborgne. Blue Ocean Strategy: How To Create Uncontested Market Space And Make The Competition Irrelevant, Harvard Business Review, 2004

Hanks, Julie de Azevedo. The Assertiveness Guide for Women: How to Communicate Your Needs, Set Healthy Boundaries & Transform Your Relationships, New Harbinger Publications, 2016.

Klontz, Brad and Ted Klontz. Mind over Money: Overcoming the Money Disorders That Threaten Our Financial Health, Broadway Books, 2009.

Morin, Christophe, Patrick Renvoise. The Persuasion Code: How Neuromarketing Can Help You Persuade Anyone, Anywhere, Anytime, John Wiley & Sons, 2018.

Rivera, Joel, and Natalie Rivera, "Life Coach Training," Transformation Academy Inc, (Worksheets received November 2019), https://transformationacademy.com/life-coach-training/.

Printed in Great Britain
by Amazon